INVISIBLE:
Surviving the Cambodian Genocide

*The Memoirs of
Mac and Simone Leng*

by Frances T. Pilch

Robert D. Reed Publishers
P.O. Box 1992
Bandon, OR 97411
Phone: 541-347-9882; Fax: -9883
E-mail: 4bobreed@msn.com
Website: www.rdrpublishers.com

Editor: Cleone Reed
Cover Designer: Cleone Reed
Book Designer: Susan Leonard

Soft-cover ISBN 13: 978-1-944297-24-4
eBook ISBN: 978-1-944297-25-1

Library of Congress Number: 2017941013

Designed and Formatted in the United States of America

DEDICATIONS

Simone and I dedicate this book
to all those who lost their lives during
the Cambodian Genocide.

~ Mac and Simone Leng

This book is dedicated to my two sons,
Rich and Lance, and their beautiful families,
and to my brother Fred and his wife Ana.
May the courage and humanity demonstrated
by Mac and Simone Leng stand as testimony
to the resilience of the human spirit,
and may their story inspire us to stand up
to tyranny and inhumanity,
in whatever form they take
in our contemporary world.

~ Frances T. Pilch

ACKNOWLEDGMENTS

This book is based on hundreds of hours of interviews of Mac and Simone Leng and members of their family. Sections in italics frame their story with the context and history of the Cambodian Genocide. Sections labeled with a name, such as "Mac, "Simone," "Mia," and "Jason" are drawn from interviews with the subjects, but written by the author.

Ann Geldzahler has been an ever-present cheerleader for this project. Members of High Plains Unitarian Church and other friends in Colorado Springs provided much appreciated support for this endeavor. Thanks also to my colleagues in Political Science at the United States Air Force Academy. I am especially grateful to Ambassador Roger Harrison and Dr. Ben Kiernan for reading the manuscript and providing such supportive and positive comments.

Some of Mac and Simone's story was recorded in filmed interviews that were designed to be the basis of a short documentary about their survival. Hal Clifford and Jason Houston of Take One Creative worked on the development of this film, and I am grateful for all the work they were able to accomplish.

I am sincerely grateful to Dr. Ryan Rich of Retina Consultants of Southern Colorado, who saved my eyesight, allowing me to complete work on the manuscript.

I am deeply indebted to Bob Reed for agreeing to publish this work when few others wanted to "take a chance" on "such a disturbing memoir." Bob's wife Cleone has been the very epitome of professionalism as she edited and formatted the manuscript. She also has a huge heart. I was very touched by Bob and Cleone's response to Mac and Simone's story. A huge thank you to Susan Leonard for making this book look exactly right!

Finally, I cannot adequately express my love and admiration for Mac and Simone and their family. I have learned so much from them about forgiveness, loyalty, resilience, and courage in the face of almost unimaginable suffering and sorrow. They have taught me how important it is to always be mindful of those who live in fear and who worry that their children will not have enough to eat. They have reminded me of how blessed we are to live in freedom and prosperity, and how appreciative we should be for the many refugees who have contributed so much to America. I will forever be indebted to them for opening my heart to understand the suffering of those who face cruelty and inhumanity. They stand with the giants in terms of their humanity. Their story is one for the ages.

TABLE OF CONTENTS

Dedications 3

Acknowledgments 5

Foreword/Editor's Note 9

Introduction 11

Chapter One
BRIEF HISTORY OF CAMBODIA 15

Chapter Two
GENOCIDE OVERVIEW 19

Chapter Three
MAC AND SIMONE'S STORY: THE BEGINNING 23

Chapter Four
CIVIL WAR 35

Chapter Five
POL POT TAKES POWER 45

Chapter Six
EVACUATION 53

Chapter Seven
DEPORTATION 59

Chapter Eight
CATERPILLAR VILLAGE 71

Chapter Nine
TAKEN AWAY 77

Chapter Ten

NEW VILLAGE, NEW BABY 87

Chapter Eleven
FLOODS 101

Chapter Twelve
THE VIETNAMESE ARRIVE 109

Chapter Thirteen
DEATH OF A BABY 117

Chapter Fourteen
ESCAPE TO THAILAND 121

Chapter Fifteen
REFLECTIONS ON LIVING UNDER THE
KHMER ROUGE 129

Chapter Sixteen
MAKING A NEW LIFE IN AMERICA 133

Epilogue 149

About the Author 155

FOREWORD/EDITOR'S NOTE

As a woman who grew up on a dairy farm in Wisconsin in a very protected cocoon (I never was exposed to the news of the outside world/Dad listened to the radio in the barn out of my earshot and I didn't watch news on TV when we got one), I grew up with messages how I should be grateful to never go to bed without supper but didn't really understand the gravity of my father's words. Until now. I now get it.

Having a Master's Degree in Education/Counseling, having worked with people who have been abused, and being a woman myself who has endured abuse, I still was not prepared to edit a book of this nature. I avoid war movies and violence on television. I find it appalling that violence sells as entertainment.

But now I am married to a man who constantly keeps up with all the news, and I can't retreat into my innocent naïve bubble anymore. Also, he publishes books on ritual abuse (I didn't know what that was either until a few years ago; they didn't teach about it in graduate school; it is way beyond the kinds of abuse I knew about), books on many social ills, and now this book, ***INVISIBLE: Surviving the Cambodian Genocide***.

Never have I been so impacted by working on a book. I told the author that I experienced PTSD in the middle of the night. My nights were punctuated with sleepless hours with my imagination riled up with images of Mac and Simone and their children living through the genocide, coupled with feelings of gratitude for our cozy flannel sheets, down comforter, wonderful pillows, and a warm house that feels comfortable and safe. I often say that I naturally live a life of gratitude, but working on this book took my gratitude to a whole new level.

When I got to one particular line in the book, I took a break and emailed the author, as follows:

> Dear Fran,
>
> I can't believe how editing your book is impacting me. I have been feeling such gratitude for all we have. Then, I just got to the end of page 101 and I have tears streaming down my face.
>
> ".... We arrived in Long Beach, California on July 21, 1979."

Never have I cried while editing a book! Until this one. I now have hopes that this book reaches students in universities and colleges world-wide to grasp the realities of our world. Genocide is still going on. I shake my head. How can this be? But it is.

This is a story of phenomenal perseverance, kindness, hard work, loyalty, and creativity in the face of day-to-day survival.

Fran Pilch, the author, spent many hours interviewing Mac and Simone (and their children) to get their profound story into this book. I can almost imagine what an emotionally wrenching experience that must have been—to reveal and relive the horrors of those three years, eight months, and twenty days—yet at the same time how healing. My admiration for Fran, for Mac, and for Simone (and their children) knows no bounds, not only for what they endured and survived but also for their lives since they came to America. What a beautiful immigrant story; that could be another book!

~ Cleone Lyvonne Reed, MSE, Editor and Graphic Designer
Author of *The Sacred Art of Clowning... and Life!*

INTRODUCTION

I first met Mow Leng in 2006 when we both were asked to speak on the topic of genocide at a panel organized by a good friend of mine, Dr. Mark Gose, at Colorado State University in Pueblo, Colorado. Mow Leng, whom I would come to know as MacKenly Leng (how he chose his American name is an interesting story in itself), was the first survivor of the Cambodian genocide I had ever met. That was not unusual. There are relatively few survivors at all, and fewer still who are willing to talk about their experiences. I was speaking about genocide as an academic who has studied mass atrocities throughout history. Mac was speaking as a survivor who had lived through one of the darkest periods of human history.

Mark told me that this was the first time that Mac had spoken publicly about the Cambodian genocide. He looked nervous, and when it was time for him to speak, he talked slowly and quietly—almost inaudibly. I was worried that he would not be able to continue, but he gained strength as he spoke. He seemed to be looking into the distance—not really seeing his audience of eager college students at all—looking into his past in an effort to understand. I remember his main question, "How could Khmer (the Cambodian people) inflict this kind of pain on each other; how could Khmer kill Khmer?" It seemed as if this question haunted him; and indeed, as I came to know Mac, I realized that he had spent tremendous time and thought trying to make sense of the almost unfathomable brutality that he and his people had endured.

I invited Mac to come to speak to my class, "War Crimes, Genocide, and Human Rights," that I had been teaching at the

United States Air Force Academy since 2000. He accepted and visited my class every fall after I met him, until I retired. I had often asked him to bring his wife Simone along, and finally, in 2012, she accompanied him. A small, beautiful woman, six years younger than Mac, she was overwhelmed to be at the Academy. I asked her if she would like to say a few words at the end of the class after Mac had spoken, and she nodded her head "no," saying that she had never spoken about the genocide that she too had endured, that she was too shy and her English was not "good enough." Nevertheless, when Mac had finished, and we had watched a segment of the film *The Killing Fields*, for which Mac had served as an advisor, I asked Simone if she had anything to add. It was as if a flood of memories came pouring from her—how she despaired of saving her children, how indeed one baby had died at her breast because she had no milk, how she, they, would have eaten anything to survive... and I knew, as I saw Mac looking at her with pride and quiet devotion, that here was a story I not only wanted to write, I had to write. Here was a story of a man and a woman who survived together, and who saved most of their family as well. Here were two people who had something to tell us about loyalty, courage, and resourcefulness. Perhaps Mac and Simone could even remind us of the abundance with which we Americans have been blessed, and the core values of character that each of us must try to understand and preserve both within ourselves and within the human community.

INVISIBLE: SURVIVING THE CAMBODIAN GENOCIDE

CHAPTER ONE

BRIEF HISTORY OF CAMBODIA

Cambodia is located in Southeast Asia; it is bordered by Vietnam to the east, Laos to the northeast, and Thailand to the northwest. The capital and largest city of Cambodia is Phnom Penh. Currently, Cambodia is a constitutional monarchy, with Hun Sen serving as the head of government. Hun Sen was associated with one branch of the Khmer Rouge that defected to Viet Nam to avoid being purged by Pol Pot, who ruthlessly eliminated all potential rivals to his authority. The current head of state is Norodom Sihamoni, a monarch chosen by the Royal Throne Council.

The Khmer Empire flourished from the 9th to the 15th centuries. Buddhism was introduced from Sri Lanka around the 13th century and became the official state religion in 1295. The Khmer Empire produced Angkor Wat, a huge pre-industrial complex whose temples remain a significant cultural treasure.

Cambodia has often been a target of its neighboring countries, especially Thailand and Viet Nam. The competition for Cambodia in the context of a Siamese-Vietnamese war in the eighteen-hundreds was a factor leading to the establishment of the French Protectorate over Cambodia. Cambodia was a protectorate of France from 1867 to 1953, as part of French Indochina. It was also occupied by the Japanese during the Second World War, from 1941 to 1945. Under King Norodom Sihanouk, Cambodia gained its independence from France in 1953.

When French Indochina gained its independence, Cambodia lost control over the Mekong Delta which was awarded to Vietnam. There are many ethnic Khmers living in this region, and it remained a point of contention between Cambodia and Vietnam. The Khmer Rouge attempt to regain control of this region was one factor leading to Vietnam's invasion of Cambodia in 1979, which deposed Pol Pot.

Although scholars disagree on the start date of the Vietnam War, significant U.S. involvement grew in the 1960's and continued until the fall of Saigon on April 30, 1975. The context of the Vietnam War is important in Cambodian history; because although King Sihanouk declared Cambodia's neutrality in the conflict, he was in fact ambivalent—sometimes allowing the U.S. to bomb North Vietnamese supply lines to the Viet Cong while also allowing the Viet Cong sanctuary within Cambodian borders. The robust American bombing campaign in Cambodia was highly destructive; and though it targeted the North Vietnamese and Viet Cong, there is no doubt that many innocent Cambodians suffered. As time went on, the King's stance turned against American involvement in Cambodia. In 1970, while he was visiting Beijing, he was ousted by a military coup led by Prime Minister General Lon Nol and Prince Sisowath Sirik Matak. The new government quickly gained support from the United States as it demanded that the Vietnamese communists leave Cambodia. This led to the civil war between the forces of the North Vietnamese and the Viet Cong and the Lon Nol military. King Sihanouk urged his countrymen to support those fighting the Lon Nol government, including the Khmer Rouge rebels.

By 1973 the Khmer Rouge had become stronger, and many of the Vietnamese-trained communists had been purged. In 1975, the Khmer Rouge launched a major offensive, and Phnom Penh fell on April 17, 1975. Upon assuming power, Pol Pot changed the official name of Cambodia to Democratic Kampuchea. The cities were immediately evacuated, and the population was sent to labor camps and rural farming projects. Everything Western was denounced; and temples, libraries, Western-oriented hospitals, and schools were destroyed. Estimates as to how many lost their lives from 1975 to 1979 range from one to three million, but most authorities cite the figure to be two million, or more than a quarter of the population of the country. Some were killed by execution, but most died from starvation, disease, and overwork.

In response to border incursions into the Mekong Delta region (which has historically been disputed territory between Cambodia and Viet Nam), Vietnamese troops, backed by the Soviets, invaded Cambodia in 1978. They took Phnom Penh in 1979, driving Pol Pot and the Khmer Rouge to the Northwest. In 1991 the Paris Comprehensive Peace Settlement was negotiated, and the United Nations was given a mandate to enforce a ceasefire, deal with refugees, and take administrative control of Cambodia until elections could be held (UNTAC—United Nations Transitional Authority in Cambodia). Pol Pot died in 1998, too soon to stand trial at the U.N.-backed war crimes tribunal, which is a hybrid tribunal designed to try major perpetrators of the Cambodian genocide. In 2001 the tribunal began its investigations in earnest, but it remains highly controversial due to its slow progress and the few perpetrators that have been convicted and sentenced. Allegations of corruption and inefficiency continue to surround the court. Eventually King Sihanouk was restored to power, but under a different governmental framework. He died in October 2012.

The Cambodian Genocide remains one of the great tragedies of the twentieth century. The country and many of its treasures were devastated and much of its infrastructure destroyed. Cambodia's ethnic minorities and professional classes were decimated, and more than one-quarter of the population lost their lives. A massive refugee crisis was created, and the country was left with extensive mine fields that have ravaged the lives of hundreds of victims. The sad legacy of the Cambodian genocide runs very deep in this beautiful, fertile country.

Skulls of Khmer Rouge Victims

CHAPTER TWO

GENOCIDE OVERVIEW

Author's Commentary

Few Americans knew much about the Cambodian genocide as it was taking place. Even now, most are familiar with the Holocaust and probably the Rwandan genocide, but the events that occurred between 1975 and 1979 in Cambodia are somewhat shrouded in mystery. The Khmer Rouge sealed the borders of Cambodia after they assumed power, and all journalists were expelled or exterminated. Until the film "The Killing Fields" was produced, general understanding of the magnitude of this atrocity was extremely limited. And yet this genocide, after the Khmer Rouge (the Red Cambodians, signifying the Maoist Communist movement) assumed power in Phnom Penh, stands as one of the most horrifying events of the Twentieth Century. More than one quarter of all Cambodians died during that time period—deliberately killed, worked to death, or from disease and starvation. Minorities were specifically targeted—in particular the Vietnamese, Cham, and Buddhist communities. Buddhists were stripped of their saffron robes, as Angkar, the name given to the governing "state" behind the Khmer Rouge, forbade the practice of religion. The country, renamed Democratic Kampuchea, descended into chaos and darkness.

The Khmer Rouge, led by Western-educated Pol Pot, embraced a radically anti-Western, agrarian ideology. They insisted upon complete devotion to Angkar. There was to be absolutely no private property.

Everyone was to labor on Angkar's behalf. Those who had been educated were suspect, and if detected, exterminated. Cities were emptied of their populations in order to move people into labor camps in the countryside. Urbanized elites, professional classes, even those who wore glasses were targeted as traitors to Angkar. Anyone connected to the former regime or the army was to be killed.

Pol Pot: May 19, 1925–April 15, 1998

The Khmer Rouge wore black shirts and pants and red scarves. Their ranks were comprised primarily of illiterate children and teenagers who could be easily manipulated by their leaders, once family ties were broken. Everyone's life was perilous; friends and relatives could betray you or you might be recognized by someone who knew you. Once identified, the Khmer Rouge would come for you at night, under cover of darkness, and take you away—never to be seen again. Easily identified targets of the Khmer Rouge were taken by the hundreds to detention centers, like the famous Tuol Sleng prison in Phnom Penh, where photographs of those held captive there and tortured until they "confessed" haunt the casual tourist to Cambodia. Of the thousands imprisoned there, almost no one escaped Tuol Sleng alive.

The population was ordered out of the cities immediately after the Khmer Rouge took power. Even hospitals were emptied of their patients, as long marches into the countryside took place. If you could not labor, you were of no use to Angkar. Human life was completely devalued. The slogan of the Khmer Rouge was, "To keep you is no benefit; to destroy you is no loss."

Foreign journalists and photographers were banned from the country and a dark curtain of invisibility descended over Cambodia. The forcible movement of the population from their homes and communities, reminiscent of the transports of the Holocaust, was calculated to disrupt the fabric of the country and to provide workers for the agrarian labor camps and other work projects of the regime.

The bombing of Cambodia by the United States during the Viet Nam War had played an important part in bringing the Khmer Rouge to power. Following the invasion of Cambodia by Viet Nam in 1979, ending the Khmer Rouge regime, the United States, stung by its loss in Viet Nam, continued to recognize the Khmer Rouge as the legitimate government of Cambodia. This persisted for several years, until Viet Nam agreed to withdraw from the country and a United Nations-run administration was put into place to monitor a governmental transition. This book, however, is not a political, but rather a personal history, of two Cambodian individuals who survived against overwhelming odds one of the worst tragedies of human history.

Mac and Simone's wedding photo, March 9, 1969, the only photograph
that survived the genocide. It was given to them
by another surviving family member.

CHAPTER THREE

MAC AND SIMONE'S STORY: THE BEGINNING

Mac

It is 2:00 a.m., and I am asleep in Pueblo West, next to my wife Simone. We have been married for almost half a century. My dreams are disturbing, and I become restless. I start to thrash, and my throat feels constricted because I cannot cry out. I must NOT cry out. I must be silent. I am being hunted—chased by faceless young men dressed in black. I am running as fast as I can, but I am weak and tired and there is no place to hide. They are closing in on me and there is no escape. They carry clubs and guns and large knives. The knives are dripping with blood. Finally, I awaken, prodded into consciousness by the gentle voice of Simone. "It's all right. You are all right. We are safe. You are in the dream." I am soaked in sweat as the dream releases me. I have had this recurrent nightmare almost every night since leaving Cambodia. My demeanor is calm and rational during my waking hours, but the terror of the genocide continues to haunt me when I sleep. I suspect it haunts us all.

In Cambodia, our family names come first. My Cambodian name is Uy Torn. That means that my last name is Uy, and Torn is my given name. My father's name was Uy Khun, and my mother was Lok Eth. They were farmers and had a big family together—eight children, of which I was the fourth, after a sister, a brother and a sister. There were four boys and four girls. Two of my sisters are still alive; one brother died during the conflict preceding the Khmer Rouge takeover, but all the rest died in the genocide. My father died of disease and starvation in 1979. We were able to save my mother, who came to the United States with Simone and me.

We grew up in a typical Cambodian house built on 9 columns or stilts. Families would live underneath the houses but sleep upstairs, to protect against animals and the elements. We lived in a very rural area, and my parents were rice farmers. I remember life as being stable and peaceful. There was always enough food for everyone. My parents worked hard, and the major threat to people was disease. Cholera was an ever-present danger, and regularly that disease would sweep over the land and take many souls with it.

Village life was full of superstitions! During a drought, we would sing and dance, praying for rain. Health care was precarious, and many women died during childbirth. If that happened, it was said that the mother's spirit would turn angry and would haunt those around her. To keep her ghost away, the villagers would paint the bottoms of clay pots with frightful faces and put the pots upside down by their front doors. A monk would be called in to cast the ghost from the house. The winds shaking the trees were also said to be ghosts! Villagers believed that dogs could sense those spirits; and indeed, the hair on the back of your neck would stand up and you would feel chilled as you passed a moaning tree. The strange, eerie screeches of birds that could only be heard—and never seen—on the darkest of nights, forewarned of death.

I guess Cambodia looks attractive to other powers, because it has been coveted by many. It was colonized by France and then occupied by Japan during World War II. Viet Nam has sought to influence Cambodia many times; our fertile, arable land is valuable to both Viet Nam and China. Some say the influence of these two countries has been the most important factor in our history. Even Thailand has laid claim to areas in Cambodia.

I was born on July 7, 1940. My dad was Buddhist and had spent time as a monk. I remember him as a good man who had no enemies. He meditated often and did not believe in killing animals, so he farmed rice. In our culture, women are expected to respect their husbands. My mother was a quiet Buddhist who worshipped my dad as if he were Buddha himself.

During the Cambodian struggle for independence, my father moved our family about twenty miles from our original home, from the jungle to Road Number 5. This road had been built by the French. My dad still went back and forth to farm, but I guess he thought it was safer for us to be in our new home. I was around three or four years old when we moved. There was a school that the French had built fairly nearby, that offered three grades. My older brother and I both went to that school, but the girls did not. At that time, girls were seldom educated. They were expected to stay at home and learn to be good mothers and wives.

My older brother was very intelligent and motivated. He finished all three grades and then went to a French-run high school, where he learned the French language. Finally, he went to Phnom Penh to get a job, but he ended up in a Technical University where he learned a valuable skill—repairing engines. Pol Pot, the leader of the Khmer Rouge, was at that Technical University also. We heard that Pol Pot studied electronics in Paris but failed in his academics and became involved with the Communist Party that was at that time, strongly influenced by Mao Tse Tung's ideology. He brought that back to Cambodia after some time spent in China.

After independence from the French, King Norodam Sihanouk was in power. He was very popular as a symbol of the Cambodian struggle against the Japanese and for independence from France. When my brother came back from France, where he also studied a technical course (he passed!), he worked for the royal family. He could fix anything, but his specialty was helicopters. He told us that the King had a dog that he adored and took everywhere with him. My brother was asked to look after the dog and take him for walks, but my brother declined to do it. He thought it was something a servant, not a professional, should do. After that, he lost favor with the King and left to join the army. I was very close to this brother, whose name was Uy Keng. I lost him in 1972. He was officially declared MIA, but he was most certainly killed in a battle against the Khmer Rouge. I will tell you that story later.

French education policy required that after finishing seventh grade, a student would go to Takeo to take a Certificate exam—sort of a high school diploma. I passed that exam, and teachers urged me to go to college in Takeo. In order to be accepted, I had to pass both a written and an oral examination in French. I passed the written exam but not the oral exam. I still remember why I failed; I had to translate the word for a little black bird, Le Merle. I didn't know it, and I didn't pass! I'll never forget that word now.

I always wanted to learn, and I desperately wanted to further my education. That has always been one of my main personal characteristics. I didn't have any money, but I left for Phnom Penh when I was sixteen, determined to succeed. For several years, my parents didn't know where I was or what I was doing. I was living with friends in the city and finding food where I could. Prah Sisovath College was a lycée in Cambodia that catered primarily to the wealthy. It was famous, and many powerful politicians sent their children there. I passed the entrance exam, classmates fed me, and I slept where I could. At the end of four years, I was ranked #15 of 120 students. It was never easy for me, because I never knew where I would sleep or who would take pity on me and feed me. But I did well and passed the test to become a teacher.

First, the Ministry of Education assigned me to teach at a small countryside school with about 300 students in a village called Krakor Pursat. If you didn't have money, they sent you away from Phnom

Penh to teach, and I definitely didn't have money! Then I passed the test to become a school principal and went back to Srok Saang, 30 kilometers southeast of Phnom Penh, to be a school administrator.

A job as school principal was prestigious in Cambodia at that time. Everyone respected education. When the Khmer Rouge took power, their policy was to kill people who were well-educated. Pol Pot wanted to erase all Western influences and return the country to the "Year Zero." It was to be as if Cambodia had no history prior to 1975, when the Khmer Rouge attained power. Youth, considered to be uncontaminated, was revered; and family loyalty was suspect. I already had one strike against me. I was in a "soft job,"—that of school principal. Soon I would have two strikes—when I became an intelligence officer in the Cambodian army. I was well educated, I was a school principal, I was literate, and I eventually worked for the Lon Nol government. I had a target on my back.

Simone

My parents were simple farmers also, but they grew corn, beans and watermelon. Sometimes my father was a fisherman too. Our family also had four girls and four boys. I was child number six, followed by two boys. My name is El Simone, because my father's name was El Bith. I was named after a nurse. My mother apparently had some Chinese blood, as do many Cambodians. I was born with light skin, and this is considered desirable in Cambodia. I was always very small, but I am also very strong and determined. Five of my brothers and sisters died in the genocide. My mother died in the genocide, but my father died when I was only eight or so.

My father was very unusual in that he wanted me to go to school to learn to read and write. I started when I was seven or eight. I did well in school; as a matter of fact, I was number one in my second-grade class. I think my dad was very fond of me. He always needed to have his ears cleaned with alcohol, and that was my job. I know it hurt him but he never complained. I loved my father very much, and losing him was very hard for me and for my whole family.

One day my cousin came running to school to tell me that my father had died. He told me not to cry, and I didn't—until I got home and saw my beloved dad wrapped in a white cloth. He died from tetanus. I remember that he had walked me to school that day; it was the first day of school that year. He was dead by the afternoon. This was a huge tragedy for my family—a mother with eight children and no way to feed them—so our family spread out to whoever would take us in.

I remember that my mother had a lady friend who asked about me. She said she knew a rich lady who would give me work and treat me well. My mother believed her, and I went with the lady friend about four hours away from my home to live with an older lady who sold fabric in a village. She had two children but lived alone. One of her children was a teacher and one was a doctor. I was to call her Auntie See.

Auntie See was extremely harsh with me and punished me all the time. My work was very strenuous for an eight-year-old. I had to start a fire in the early morning, carry a heavy pail of water, put the pot on, and make soup to sell. This lady was a Chinese woman who had married a Cambodian. My mother had wanted me to continue going to school, but there was no time to do homework, so my education came to a halt. I had to clean and debone fish, grind flour, chop cilantro, and thicken soup. I was never idle from dawn until night. I worked all the time and was exhausted when I lay down to sleep.

I remember clearly one time that I made a mistake. During the rainy season, we collected rainwater in clay pots. We called the rain "good water from the sky." Auntie had three clay pots. I filled and carried two, but I broke the third. I remember she beat me with a stick on my naked skin. I was never quite sure what Auntie See thought about me, but she used to tell me often how beautiful I was. She would raise my shift when I was lying asleep and tell me that I was perfect and that any man I married would be very lucky, all the while stroking my private parts. I never told anyone.

One time her daughter came home and brought me a new dress. I was told to sleep on the floor, and I had a mat and pillow and blanket. At 6:00 or 7:00, when it was dark, we would go to sleep. The son was there also, but outside the room. I woke up as the son was trying to rape me. My pants were down and he had his leg between my legs. But I made so much noise that he left me alone and was not able to finish. I have never told anyone before about the old lady and her hands and her son who tried to rape me. It was a terrible time for me, full of fear and very hard labor.

For two years, my mother never came to see me, and she never knew of my terrible existence. The one thing I did have was the occasional new dress. But the work was excruciating and hard, and I was often punished. Finally, my dad's mother came and asked me if I wanted to go home; so, I went home with grandmother and never told anyone.

The second oldest sister in my family asked my mother if I could come and live with her. She never had children but had a nice, clean, well organized home. I went to school again while I was with her. My brother-in-law was old but considered well to do. He had a job as a construction director. He died before the Khmer Rouge took power. My sister's name was Bopha, which means flower. Eventually she remarried a man who worked in customs. The Khmer Rouge killed them both.

But even though I was living with my sister, my life was not easy. She was very strict. I don't remember much about those months except one incident. I came home from school and I was very hungry. I cooked some fish but burned it accidentally. It was to be supper for everyone. My sister was so angry that I had burned it that she hit me with the tongs that were used to pick up hot charcoal. She beat me so hard that a neighbor had to intervene to rescue me. I remember the neighbor rubbing salve on the burns. I spent three years with Bopha, until finally my mother came and took me home.

My education stopped in the seventh grade, when my mother married a widower with four children. My mother said, "You're a girl; you don't need more education." I moved back with my mother to help take care of the children. My stepfather worked hard to support the family. He was strict, but we did have food to eat and clothes to wear. I lived there until I was sent to cook for my brother in Phnom Penh.

Living with my brother was wonderful. He wanted me to learn a trade, so he sent me to sewing school. My brother and I shared a house with two unmarried ladies. I was safe; and although I worked hard, I loved learning how to sew. Every day I walked several kilometers to the sewing classes.

One day while I was walking to school, two guys on a motorcycle blocked my way. I guess I was 17 years old at the time. I ran away from them, but my brother, when he heard the story, gave me a brand new bicycle that I rode every day to school. He also paid me a small amount of money for working for him. To me, that was a lot of money! I felt as if I was developing into an independent and skilled woman.

While I was going to sewing school, I made a beautiful wedding dress for my sister. I took the dress to my village, and other clothes I had made also, to show my family. They lived across the street from the school where Mac worked. It was the first time that Mac saw me. I guess he was attracted to me right then and there. I was 18 and Mac was 24, and Mac was looking for a wife. In Cambodia, we have people who arrange marriages between families. Mac had a representative approach my sister, who lived in the village, about an arrangement. My sister told him to speak to my mother. I think my mom was pretty happy to think that someone was interested in marrying me! It would solve a lot of problems about my future.

My mother came to Phnom Penh to tell me that she had had a visitor. "Someone wants to marry you," she said. As would any young girl, I asked her, "What does he look like?" I remember that my mother said, "Not too tall, not too short." I asked about his skin color. She said, "Not too light, not too dark." I asked what his work was. "High School principal." What about his nose? Was it flat or regular looking?" "Just normal looking." So I told my mother to ask about his family.

The representative told us that he came from a good family, and like a good intermediary, she also told his family that my family was respectable. Our mutual parents got together to meet and to discuss what the groom would pay for me. In this case, it was fruit, clothing, and some gold. Gold was like money at that time in Cambodia. Later, under the Khmer Rouge, there was no money. Gold had no value; but if you were found with it in your possession, you would be killed, and the gold would be given to Angkar.

I did not speak to Mac at all before we were married. We did go out on one "date." I think you would find it funny to hear about what that date was like. We were not allowed to go alone together, so my sister and brother- in-law came along. I sat on the far left, my sister and brother-in-law in the middle, and Mac on the far right.

As the wedding day approached, I became terrified. I didn't want to get married. An old Chinese lady lived upstairs. She checked out Mac for me and said that he wore navy pants and a white shirt and rode a Vespa. I said, "My mother told me that he had neither dark nor light skin. She didn't tell me the truth! I told my mother I didn't want to marry a dark-skinned man." The Chinese lady spoke very wise words. She said, "Dark skin, light skin, it doesn't matter. As long as he has a good heart. He is a school principal and a teacher. He will be a good husband." We were married on March 9, 1967.

I went to live with Mac in his village, about two hours southeast of Phnom Penh. The village was called Saang Preak Toch. School was about fifteen minutes by scooter for Mac, and we lived with his two brothers. It didn't take long for us to have our first baby. Leng Ma, or Mia, was born in 1967; Leng Man, or Jason in 1969; Leng Mara in 1972, and then in 1978 we had a little boy who lived only six months and died while we still lived under the Khmer Rouge. He was named Leng Banana Root for the banana root that kept us alive when we had nothing to eat. From 1975 on, I had no periods, which is common in starving women; therefore, there was no way to know that I would get pregnant with my Banana Root baby. I didn't think I could, but there he was!

Giving birth to our first-born Mia was exciting and a time of hope for us. There were no doctors and no birthing classes. A pregnant lady would have a nurse come and help. I remember that a neighbor corralled Mac one day and said that she thought I was about to have the baby. Mac had to leave on his Vespa to go and get the nurse. The nurse was about 50 years old and also drove a scooter. She took one look at me and said, "You are so small and skinny. Don't go anywhere."

She instructed everyone to open all the lids on pots and pans and bottles. That's an old cultural tradition to let bad spirits escape. Then everyone had to pray and burn incense. She made me a potion of Chinese herbs to drink to help with the pain. I remember taking three very deep breaths and pushing hard. Mia was born! Mac's two brothers lived with us at that time while they were going to school. One said, "Give me my niece." The other one said, "Oh, she looks just like me!" These brothers were very close to each other and so loving toward me. The Khmer Rouge killed them both.

I was a new wife with a new baby. The real problems started in 1970 when Cambodia was completely chaotic due to civil war and an invasion by the Viet Cong. There was fighting everywhere. Roads were closed and villages were under siege. The night was full of the sounds of gunfire, and the sky lit up with flares and rockets. I feared that peace would not surround us again for a long, long time.

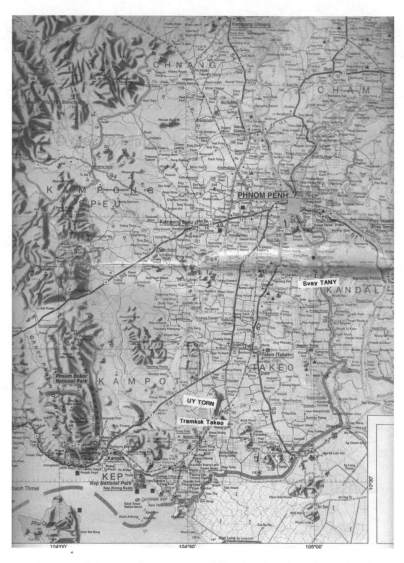

A map of the southern part of Cambodia, their homeland

CHAPTER FOUR

CIVIL WAR

Mac

In 1970, General Lon Nol came to power by military coup. He overthrew King Sihanouk, who fled to China. When the Royalists were deposed by the Lon Nol regime, everything changed very fast. The Khmer Rouge, which had been only a small group of fighters, emerged very quickly, gaining supporters, and taking territory. They were supported by the Viet Cong. It became very difficult and dangerous to run the school. There was no stability and calm. The Viet Cong and some Khmer Rouge elements were infiltrating our village. Some of the Lon Nol army was near the village also. I knew that a huge conflict was inevitable.

One day I had to go to Phnom Penh, and by the time I returned, at 9:00 in the morning, the Viet Cong army was between me and my school. Simone had not come with me, because Mia was only twelve months old, and she wanted to stay at home with her. By 3:00 in the afternoon, the Lon Nol army was shooting rockets into our village, which had been further infiltrated by the Viet Cong and Khmer Rouge. The B40 rockets produced 1500-degree heat. Everything was burning. There was a river between the Lon Nol army and the Viet Cong army on the other side. I couldn't get to my wife and our baby.

Simone

Everything was chaos. We lived in a tiny unit in a small row of rooms next to our landlord. When the rockets started, I grabbed Mia and we hid under a concrete basin. One of the rockets hit a wood factory nearby, and pieces of the bombs and wood fragments fell inside the basin, which was in the middle of the house. There was a twelve-year-old girl who lived with us at the time. Her name was Kapoch, and she helped me with the baby. Kapoch was hysterical. We stayed under the basin from 3:00 p.m. until late at night—probably 10:00 p.m., through the bombs, the fires, and the bullets. It was all I could do to calm Mia and Kapoch and keep them safe. Several groups of fighters came by. First the Viet Cong and then another group. We weren't sure exactly who they were.

My next-door neighbor called softly to us and urged us to come to her side of the house. Interestingly, she had three beautiful daughters and had really hoped that Mac would choose to marry one of them. Even though he chose me instead of one of those girls, she and I became friends. I crawled to her home carrying Mia, and Kapoch followed. After that, many of us, including the neighbors, the landlord and his four daughters, and a big dog, were hiding under a bed. I had nothing with me—only a scarf and a key. Around 2:00 a.m., there was a knock on the door and a soldier, probably Viet Cong, told us that everyone had to get out or we would be hit by bombs at sunrise.

We ran to an old canal that no longer held water. I remember there were tree thorns everywhere, and we had no shoes. My feet were ripped apart by the thorns, and my sarong was completely torn. We ran past the zone of the fighting and up to a rice field. I just sat there, under a palm tree, until a Viet Cong army guy who spoke Khmer came along and told me to "go further." We did, but by the morning we were very hungry. We hadn't eaten all day! We sat down, and

I tried to figure out a way to make some soup for Mia when a bomb went off right next to me. We got up again and kept running. That night we found an abandoned hut. We all climbed up and slept.

The old man and his daughters were still with me, as well as my little maid. The dog had long since run away. We had no idea if we would survive the night, but dawn came and we were all safe. We got up and kept walking to the west. One day a man came riding by on a bicycle. It turned out that he was my "godfather," who had sort of adopted me after Mac and I were married. He said, "Mac came looking for you, but he couldn't get close to your old house." He took me to Mac, and the little maid left to find her family. Kapoch became a Khmer Rouge fighter. Three years later, after the genocide had started, she found Mac and me and brought us some rice and fish. She never betrayed us, and we don't know what happened to her.

Mac

I could not go back to the village where I had been the school principal because the town was now occupied by the Viet Cong. The school where I had worked was only 30 kilometers from the Vietnamese border. My future was very insecure. It didn't look as if being a school principal was going to be the solution. We moved our little family to Phnom Penh and literally started over with nothing. How was I going to support my family? I decided to join the army. The army sent me to a military academy for six months, which isn't really a lot of time for training. I did learn a little bit about using weapons. I never saw any Americans there. If there were American troops in Cambodia at that time, I did not see them, although there was an Embassy.

Simone

We literally had nothing when we started our life anew in Phnom Penh. Things had calmed down a little by then, and a road had been reopened to where we used to live. We decided to go back, collect our belongings, and return to our apartment. When we found our old home, it had been looted. Our pots and pans were gone, and only a few of our clothing items were still there. But they had not taken my sewing machine, and we took it with us to the city. I guess none of the looters knew how to sew! But I had been to sewing school, so the sewing machine was incredibly valuable to me. I started a small tailor shop in the city.

By that time everyone was trying to get out of the war zones in the countryside and into Phnom Penh. The city was crowded with displaced people and families. The Colonel for whom Mac worked found Mac a post in the city, but things were falling apart. I remember that while I was trying to make a little money with the sewing, I became pregnant with Jason. After a few months, Mia became very seriously ill; and I sold almost everything I had to pay doctors and buy medicine for her. She had boils all over; she couldn't sleep. It took a long time before she got better, and about that time Jason was born. Things were hard. We had been fairly well off and secure when Mac was a principal. Now we sensed that everything was shifting. We weren't exactly sure how, but we knew the changes were making life harder and more dangerous.

Mac

We lived in a little apartment in the middle of the city. Our second child Jason was born there. After the military training, I was sent to work with the Cambodian army about 50 kilometers north of Phnom Penh. In that job, I supervised 120 men even though

I was only a lieutenant. One day in the battlefield, I had to go to the command post to fix one of my radios, called PRC10 and PRC 25, and American made. While waiting, the chief of the post, who was a colonel, asked me if I knew how to write a military message in French. He gave me some old ones to work with, and I tried. I wrote to the Phnom Penh command, "We need troops and ammunition due to a deteriorating situation." I wrote in French rather than Khmer so that the Viet Cong would be less capable of understanding it. When the message was sent successfully, the colonel asked me to stay with him and work on military messages as my job. Col Ngin Saroeurng changed the course of my life by giving me this opportunity. Also, I was safer with this new occupation, as I was not in the thick of the fighting.

At this time, Americans were bombing in the East, the Khmer Rouge was coming toward Phnom Penh mainly from the Northwest, and the Viet Cong were supporting the Khmer Rouge and coming up from the south. The Viet Cong and Khmer Rouge never fought in the daylight. They were very good at fighting in the dark and in the rain. Lon Nol's military was paid to fight; the Khmer Rouge and Viet Cong fought viciously because they believed in their cause. Their morale was high and they acted like a revolutionary movement. They would stay and fight at times when the Lon Nol military might run away. I believed in republican government. I was educated, and I supported the Lon Nol government because I believed in the system, even though corruption was rampant. The vast majority of the Khmer Rouge were illiterate. They had no wives and no property. They were young. They felt they had nothing to lose, and they believed in their cause.

Phnom Penh was becoming more and more unstable. The Viet Cong had already infiltrated the city. We lived alongside them often without knowing it. We all look alike, and many of them spoke Khmer. There was no street fighting, but I knew the situation was deteriorating.

I had become quite well-respected in the army and certainly important to the Colonel. In 1972, I was sent to Viet Nam to take an intelligence course. When Mara was born in 1972, I was in Viet Nam learning about intelligence operations. The school was inside a huge training center and was run by the Vietnamese. At the time, both Cambodia and South Viet Nam were fighting the Viet Cong. At this training school, I met many Americans; and even though the training was done by the Vietnamese, I was able to see how an American intelligence office worked.

After Saigon, I went home to Phnom Penh and worked for the same boss, the Colonel. Sometimes I was posted out in the field. One night, shortly after I had returned from Viet Nam, I was in a command post with two commanders, three captains, and myself, all sleeping. The Khmer Rouge attacked our post, and there was intense fighting. After one or two hours of combat, the Khmer Rouge ran away into the night. In the morning, we discovered than many soldiers had been killed. Trenches were lined with their bodies. The Khmer Rouge usually wore black shirts and pants, but sometimes they wore no shirts. One of the great difficulties in a war like that is identifying the enemy. How could you tell if a soldier was with you or against you?

Soon I was promoted to Chief of Intelligence Officer of the State. For six months, I taught interrogation techniques to army personnel, and I conducted many interrogations myself. I was opposed to using any torture techniques. Sometimes I think that the reason my life was spared during the genocide was that I never did anything against my fundamental moral code. I was not corrupt; I could not be bribed; and I never abused my prisoners. I never violated the laws of war.

At that time, the army was capturing many Khmer Rouge fighters from the battlefield, young girls as well as young men. I made sure that their privacy was never violated. That Khmer Rouge army was mostly comprised of teenagers who believed that they were fighting the Americans. They had been taught to think that this was a war against American imperialism. I never sent these young people to Marshall Court. If they had gone to the court, they would have ended up in a Phnom Penh prison. I always tried to persuade my boss to release them when the interrogations were finished. Maybe they went back to fight some more; but we could not feed them, so I didn't think it was right to keep them. I knew they would not survive long in a prison—especially the young women.

We received a lot of valuable information from these young fighters. My tactic was simple—I befriended them. To get good information, I felt they had to like me. They would be interrogated in the morning, and then in the evening I would visit them personally and bring them food. I felt that if I could reason with them, they would not return to the Khmer Rouge. Some of my intelligence officers would go out into the countryside in civilian clothes to discern the intentions of the Khmer Rouge. Then we could prepare our troops for what was to come. I became more and more aware of the strength of this revolutionary movement and was soon convinced that the Lon Nol government could not survive.

For one thing, corruption in the Lon Nol military ran very deep. For example, a battalion was supposed to be comprised of 512 men; therefore, money was allocated for 512 men. But in reality, perhaps there were only 115 men! Someone, probably a commander, would be pocketing the extra pay. I did receive regular pay, and I believe that by the time I was working primarily as an interrogator, the Cambodian army was financed by the Americans. So, maybe that was my first "American" job!

An officer who had first noticed me, Col Ngin Saroeung, was very instrumental in my life. He was good to me, and I worked for him for a long time. We knew each other well. When we were both forced out of Phnom Penh by the Khmer Rouge we saw each other.

He was sitting in the back seat of an old Mercedes and his wife was in the front. They had no gas and were surrounded by Khmer Rouge. His last act of kindness to me was to look the other way and show no glimmer of recognition. I needed to be invisible to survive. I will always be grateful to him for that final act of kindness.

Mac

In 1973, the United States was bombing Cambodia heavily. Daily radio broadcasts carrying the voice of Sihanouk urged the people to go into the jungle and fight against the Lon Nol army. By 1973 the Khmer Rouge controlled two-thirds of the country and more than half of the population. As masses of humanity streamed into Phnom Penh to escape the war zones, the Lon Nol regime was collapsing.

One of the great tragedies of my life was the loss of my older brother. He and I were very close. He was also in the military, and in 1974 he commanded three battalions in the field to the northeast of Phnom Penh. During an especially intensive time of fighting, I was on the northwest side of a river and he was on the northeast. The battle raged around him for twelve days and thirteen nights. After that battle he was listed as "missing in action," and I never saw him again or knew exactly what happened. But I did hear his last words on my radio. He said, "Here they come. I have to go."

He had been posted at a temple, and I think he had about 700 men fighting for him at the time. The Khmer Rouge had surrounded them, and he was desperate for more ammunition and air support. Without that help, he knew he and his men would be doomed. I knew it too, and I raced to Phnom Penh to see the generals and pleaded with them to send my brother aid. I said, "Please help my brother. He cannot win without this help."

For twelve days, there had been absolutely no troops to relieve him. The generals did send some airplane flares to illuminate the treacherous nights. As I have told you, the Khmer Rouge fighters were especially active and skilled in the dark and in the rain. I had begged the generals and commanders to send airplanes and artillery to save my brother and his troops from sure defeat. They assured me that they would and told me not to worry. However, no airplanes were sent to help. Finally, I was able to get one of our friends to supply some troops to go to my brother's rescue. Desperate to help my brother, I went with them. We got to the wide river; I was on one side with four or five big boats; my brother and his troops were at the temple on the other side, besieged by the Khmer Rouge. This was October or November; the current in the river was extremely strong and the rain was torrential. The soldiers would not get on the boats. They were terrified and unwilling to obey me because I was not their official boss. I drew my gun and yelled at them to "get on the boats." By then it was sunset and everyone was drenched and freezing cold in the wind. I telephoned my friend, who ordered some artillery fire from the Little Mountain (a two-piece artillery gun) to cover them. Finally, the men got on the boats, but as they crossed the river, they were massacred by fire from B 40 guns made by the Chinese. No boats made it. All those men perished.

It was 10:00 p.m. and we again called for air support. We were told an airplane would come and help, but the planes were escorting rice from Batt Dunbung to Phnom Penh, and no plane ever came. I stood helplessly, with a river between us as my brother made his last radio call. All I remember is that I took my radio and smashed it into pieces and cried. I remained terribly bitter for a long time toward the generals who had promised to help and who then betrayed me. Later, when I was back in the capitol, many families came and asked me what had happened to their sons. I had to tell them that they were all dead. I had to tell my own family that our brother was missing. But

I knew better. I was to live with the guilt of not being able to save my brother for the rest of my life. I had to live with the knowledge of the drowned soldiers. I know what tragedy is.

Mac

Do I miss Cambodia? Thunder always makes me homesick. Cambodia seems very far away. I love America. Simone and I are both American citizens and have worked extremely hard to succeed in this country. But I do miss the sounds of nature in Cambodia—the thunder would mean rain, and then when the rain would stop, you would hear crickets. Crabs would run out of puddles. In Cambodia, when I was a child, if there was a drought, people in a village would sit under a tree and pray for rain. They believed that an angel or spirit could give them rain. But usually the rains didn't come, except in the rainy season. When the rains DID come, it was a time of sweetness. You would hear the sound of rain on the palm leaf roofs. Click, click, click. The thunder was loud, or soft, or slow. I think of Cambodia every time I hear the rain.

During the Viet Nam war, Americans would drop bombs from B-52s on Cambodia. Series of bombs would sound like thunder, and when the bombs exploded there would be flashes like lightning. And there would be great shaking. Therefore, thunder and lightning mean many things to me. Not all sweetness.

CHAPTER FIVE

POL POT TAKES POWER

Mac

How did the Khmer Rouge come to take power in Cambodia? It happened very fast. The Khmer Rouge grew from a small band of jungle guerrillas to a powerful movement in the matter of a year or two, and American involvement in Viet Nam had a lot to do with the way things unfolded. King Sihanouk allowed the North Vietnamese to use Cambodia through the Ho Chi Minh trail, which was a supply route from North Vietnam, partially through Cambodia, to South Vietnam. He also allowed the Americans to bomb North Vietnamese camps in the border regions of Cambodia.

The bombings by B-52s of Cambodia were devastating and terrifying. The American military was bombing targets 50 or 60 kilometers from Phnom Penh. We could see the flashes from the bombs, like lightening, illuminate the sky in the distance, followed by the "Boom, Boom, Boom" of the explosions. The ground would shake. At one time, Simone was living with her sister very close to one area where the bombs were being dropped. Villages were destroyed and many Cambodians displaced. Thousands were homeless and fled towards the cities. Some were recruited by the Khmer Rouge. The bombing provided the Khmer Rouge with fertile ground for anti-American propaganda.

Author's Commentary

Between March 1969 and August 1973, the United States bombed Cambodia in a campaign called Operation Menu—beginning with Operation Breakfast, named for the meeting at which Henry Kissinger and President Nixon had developed the secret campaign. It was designed to eliminate Viet Cong sanctuaries in Cambodia, but this goal proved to be elusive. In April 1970, the President ordered an incursion by U.S. and South Vietnamese troops into Cambodia to attack Viet Cong strongholds. This incursion was about a month after the coup that displaced Sihanouk and replaced him with the Lon Nol regime. In the B-52 campaign, hundreds, if not thousands, of Cambodians were killed or displaced, their homes and villages destroyed.

Mac

Sihanouk was trying to placate both sides, all the while claiming to be neutral. At some point, America withdrew support from Sihanouk, and the coup by Lon Nol took place. I can't imagine that the coup succeeded without American backing. Sihanouk had become very friendly with China, and at that time, China was America's enemy. He also was unwilling to give the United States' effort in the Viet Nam war unconditional support. The Lon Nol government that took over was corrupt and incompetent.

When Sihanouk was deposed, he fled to China. Apparently, Pol Pot talked to him there. At the time, Sihanouk was very popular in Cambodia. Everyone had photographs and pictures of the king! The Khmer Rouge detested the idea of a monarchy and the royalists; but when Lon Nol overthrew the King and it became apparent that the new government would be very pro-American, they decided to support Sihanouk and rally the country through his message of liberating Cambodia from foreign influence. Every day there would be broadcasts on Peking Radio, calling for the Cambodian people to go into the jungles and fight against Lon Nol to restore the throne to Sihanouk. The Lon Nol government was ostensibly republican, but it was also extremely corrupt, and it received a lot of support from the United States. The U.S. expected it would receive support in the Viet Nam conflict in return.

At the time, I was no longer working as a military intelligence officer. The situation in the countryside had become dire, and it was clear that the Lon Nol forces were losing as Phnom Penh became surrounded. It was only a matter of time! I was filing documents for the Cambodian Senate. The command posts had been abandoned.

I was well-educated, and though I could not know details about what was to come, I did know that a communist regime would bring many changes to our country. One night I sat with my parents and wife and told them I believed the Lon Nol forces were losing, and that under communism our lives would be very different. I told them that we would no longer be free to move about or to choose our lifestyle. We would not be able to eat what we wanted—maybe even live where we wanted. I told my parents that I thought we should take the opportunity to leave that night and escape to Thailand before the city fell and communist rule took effect. My mother absolutely rejected this idea. She said it was ridiculous to think that we would not be able to eat what we wanted! Cambodia had many fertile rice fields! She didn't want to leave the security of her home and the places she knew. In Cambodian culture, one's respect for and obedience to one's parents is fundamental. We did not leave, and the city fell.

Many people blame Prince Sihanouk for the genocide in Cambodia. However, he was an enigma. He built Cambodia, but he also helped destroy Cambodia. The Khmer Rouge would not have been as effective without Sihanouk calling for the Cambodian people to support his return to power. He died in 2012, and many people in the countryside still revere him as the godfather of the country. I believe he was first a nationalist and a royalist, but then became strongly influenced by China. China has always been interested in our country, as has Viet Nam.

In the beginning, there were three different groups of the Khmer Rouge movement. The first was the group led by Pol Pot— rabidly Maoist and very closely tied to China. The second we could call Khmer Rouge Patriotic. It was led by Hou Yon and Hou Nim. Eventually, this group number two was eliminated by Pol Pot, and Hou Yon and Hou Nim were killed. Pol Pot was ruthless in eliminating rivals in the revolutionary movement. Group three was the Khmer Rouge closely associated with the Viet Minh. Hun Sen, who was part of this group, is still in the Cambodian government. These three groups joined together to fight against the Lon Nol government. After their victory, Pol Pot consolidated power, eliminated group two, and would probably have killed Hun Sen but for the fact that he defected to North Viet Nam. Eventually, he was to return to Cambodia when the Vietnamese invaded and defeated Pol Pot on January 1, 1979. Hun Sen is now the Prime Minister of Cambodia.

Lon Nol was supported by South Vietnamese troops, but they were so occupied with fighting in Viet Nam itself that their presence in Cambodia was minimal. However, the Viet Cong were supporting the Khmer Rouge and had many troops in Cambodia. Pol Pot was supported by China and Sihanouk. On April 17, 1975, Pol Pot took Phnom Penh. Even though King Sihanouk had implored the Cambodian people through radio broadcasts from China to fight against Lon Nol with the revolutionary Khmer Rouge in the jungle, once Pol Pot took Phnom Penh the King did not rule Cambodia. He was virtually under house arrest while Pol Pot consolidated the country. The Khmer Rouge ruled Cambodia for three years, eight months, and twenty days. Oddly, though, when the Khmer Rouge took Phnom Penh, we didn't even know the name of Pol Pot. Maybe some people did, but I did not. The Khmer Rouge were simply thought of as communist revolutionaries who opposed the Lon Nol government and its ties to the Americans. We didn't really know much about their ideology.

We did hear very quickly of "Angkar." Angkar was the name for the new regime or state. It was said that "Angkar has lots of eyes, like the pineapple." Nobody could hide anything from Angkar. As time went on we started to understand more about the ideology behind the Khmer Rouge.

The most important principles of Khmer Rouge ideology were the idea of the "year zero," its radical Maoist orientation, and its stridently anti-Western stance. Within a very short time of assuming power, all of the schools, hospitals, courts, and religious institutions were destroyed. Lawyers, doctors, teachers, and wealthy property owners were exterminated. People who wore glasses or had the soft hands of the professional classes were eliminated. Buddhists were killed or forced to abandon their robes. All private property now belonged to the state, and everyone was driven from urban areas into the countryside into forced labor camps. Only very young children were allowed to stay with families. Everyone had to work, even fairly young children of six or seven, and mothers. All ties to the former culture of Cambodia were to be severed; there were to be no foreign influences permitted, and everything and everyone was to belong to Angkar. There was no history—no culture. This was the "year zero," the beginning of everything under the new regime of Pol Pot.

Money and banking were eliminated. All the valuable things you possessed were either taken away from you or no longer had any worth. There was no way to communicate—no newspapers or radios. The only way one could know what was happening was through talking to others. Those conversations were very dangerous; there were spies everywhere. It was safer to remain silent, devoid of knowledge, devoid of money, with only your intuition and intelligence to guide you.

At around 7:00 a.m. on the day that the Khmer Rouge took over Phnom Penh, everyone lined the streets to welcome them. There was no street fighting. The Lon Nol army simply gave up. The Khmer Rouge were not viewed with suspicion. When they walked into the city, people clapped and cheered. They weren't even known as the Khmer Rouge at that time. Khmer Rouge actually means "Red Cambodians." Red stood for communist; they also wore red scarves. Khmer is another word for "Cambodian." They entered from the West, North, and East. The message that everyone heard and believed was that these revolutionaries would bring peace and an end to conflict. The war would be over, and therefore they were welcomed into the city.

I knew something about communist ideology, but what took me by surprise were the orders to evacuate the cities. This was completely unexpected. In a matter of an hour or less, everything changed. Khmer Rouge with guns went to every house and ordered everyone out. If someone did not obey, he was shot. I myself quickly observed people being searched for weapons and then shot on the spot. Everyone was ordered to leave Phnom Penh immediately and take nothing with them. They said this was only temporary—that you didn't need to take anything because "in a few days, you will be back." This was facilitated by propaganda. We were all told that the Americans were about to bomb the city, and therefore, we had to evacuate. Long lines of persons and carts flowed from the city in three main directions—West, North, and South. We didn't know much; all we were told was to leave and keep going. Khmer Rouge soldiers with weapons presided over the exodus. Even hospitals had to empty out; patients were on stretchers and in wheelchairs. Some were still attached to IVs. You were told which way to go, and you couldn't change directions unless ordered to. You were headed to toil in labor camps organized by the Khmer Rouge, but we didn't even know that at the time.

When I heard the evacuation orders and saw the chaos, I put an AK47 and a pistol under the hood of my car, which I thought I would take to evacuate my family. Then I saw the Khmer Rouge shoot people for owning guns. I quickly decided not to take the car! Instead, we took two bicycles. Our little group was comprised of Simone, our three children (Mia, Jason, and Mara), my little brother who was married with a baby, two of my sisters, and myself.

CHAPTER SIX

EVACUATION

Simone

We knew a male nurse who had come home from the civil war. He had a lot of medicine in a bag with him. When I heard the evacuation commands, I immediately ran to him and bought everything he would sell me—four syringes, antibiotics, diarrhea medicine, and more. I hid all of this underneath rice in various bags. Eventually, that medicine was to save our lives; and the money spent to buy it was no longer good for anything in Cambodia under the Khmer Rouge.

Mac was wearing a watch as we left. There were checkpoints along the evacuation routes where people were searched, questioned, and sometimes killed. At one of the checkpoints, a Khmer Rouge soldier saw it and ordered him to take it off, which he did. There was no need for a watch anymore, as Angkar even controlled time. From then on there were no watches or clocks. Everyone was stealing and looting during the evacuation, but Mac and I refused to do that. I also had a little jewelry and gold that I hid in a rice bag. If it had been discovered, I would have been killed, and it would have been confiscated for Angkar.

Eventually, the Khmer Rouge would adopt a policy of moving populations about every six months in forced transports. Because you were not allowed to own anything, you were empty handed except for what you had hidden; therefore, you were completely dependent on those who herded you around. There was to be absolutely no private property—only the clothes on your back.

Mia

As a young girl, I remember when Pol Pot's Khmer Rouge invaded our homeland. I heard gun shots and bombs going off all night till the sun came up. The Khmer Rouge went door to door knocking. They told us we had to leave the house. My parents left all the important documents and pictures behind. Dad was a smart man. He had been a teacher and a high-ranking military officer. He knew history and how the communist mind worked; consequently, he didn't want any evidence of who he was going with us. We didn't take much, pretty much just took the clothes on our backs and a pot of marinade chicken Mom had made from the night before. I thought it was just us, but once we got to the main road, there were other families and people sitting along the side of the road.

There were men, women, and children all crying, running around looking for their families. My parents told us, if anyone asked what Dad did for a living, just say you don't know or say he's a farmer, and sure enough they did ask. They said they were looking for doctors, teachers, lawyers, and other professionals—the educated people. They told them they were going to take them to a special place to help other people. They made it sound important so that those people would step forward. I heard that the ones that did step forward were lined up and shot.

Mac

We left Phnom Penh in a long caravan of people on an unnumbered road, almost directly South. My parents left to the North on Road #4. After heading south, we crossed to the east, toward the village where I had been principal, in order to find Simone's sister.

By then we were very hungry, and we felt that we could find more food in the village where I used to serve as principal. Once in the village, we labored on a communal farm, mostly hoeing rice and corn. Sometimes my job was to cut down trees. My sister-in-law watched the little children, as she had a young baby. Simone also worked in the fields. Laborers were separated by gender and by age. Simone and I, therefore, worked in different areas. At that time, the labor supervisor was just someone from the village. We saw very few Khmer Rouge there, but whenever we did, I kept a very low profile. I kept my head down and my eyes averted hoping no one would notice me. I tried to be invisible. We stayed in that village for about six months.

The Khmer Rouge roughly divided the population into three groups. There were the "17 Group" (those who were evacuated from the cities on April 17, 1975), the "Originals" (those who lived in the villages and rural areas all their lives), and "Angkar" (representatives of the new regime, including the Khmer Rouge soldiers). Angkar believed in elevating the poorest to more power and depriving the former elites of all power. Therefore, the Originals were used to administer villages, the 17 Group was always suspect, and Angkar ruled mysteriously, as from behind a veil. We were labeled as part of the "17 group." Therefore, we were potentially enemies of Angkar. If we were believed to be important or educated in our past lives, we would have to be executed. For the next three years, we had to lose ourselves and become invisible. We had to blend in, pretend ignorance, and disguise who we really were.

In the village where I used to be the principal, however, many former teachers, parents, and students knew us. The net of the Khmer Rouge administration was not drawn tightly for the first few months, though. Still, if anyone had pointed us out to a Khmer Rouge soldier, we would have been killed. No one betrayed us. Nevertheless, food was very scarce and my family was always hungry.

We were not allowed to cultivate or own food privately. Everything belonged to Angkar.

Cambodia is one of the most fertile countries in the world. We had abundant crops of rice. You might well ask why so many thousands starved to death under the Khmer Rouge. The answer is that no one was permitted to cultivate their own crops. Once rule was consolidated, everyone had to eat in communal cafeterias where food was extremely minimal and handed out only to those who worked to the Khmer Rouge's satisfaction. Where did all the cultivated rice go? I suspect it went straight to China where it was traded for weapons. Of course, the Khmer Rouge soldiers and accomplices were well-fed. Often we were given only two cups of rice per day for a family of seven. When I say that we were given porridge, it was not porridge as you might know it. Porridge consisted of a watery substance with very little grain or anything of nutritional value.

We also had no salt, which in a hot climate is essential for wellbeing. My cousin was taken from his parents when he was only twelve to slave in salt fields on the coastline of Cambodia. He was in a group of other young Cambodians who labored from sunrise to sunset under intolerable conditions from which there was no escape. The father of my cousin, Roun Ney, was imprisoned by the Khmer Rouge. Roun Ney was then separated forcibly from his parents and sent to the labor camps. He never saw his mother again, bur remarkably, he and his father survived.

What happened to all the rice and salt that the enslaved populations produced? My cousin says that trucks came and took the salt away, and they never knew where it was headed. We knew that Khmer Rouge leadership had access to good food produced by the laborers. We believe that both salt and rice was shipped to China to trade for weapons for the regime.

There was a wealthy man in the village called Sroy. He had two sons, one of whom named Ev, was a Khmer Rouge soldier. One day Sroy took me quietly and showed me a canoe that was hidden in a rice bush behind my old school. He then told me where we could find water lilies. He knew that Simone and I were starving. This was a very dangerous enterprise because the canoe belonged to the Khmer Rouge. Nevertheless, before dawn I stealthily took the canoe and gathered lilies for Simone to barter.

Simone

In Cambodia, people who sell lilies, as I did, from place to place, were the poorest of the poor. I didn't sell the lilies for money. Money no longer meant anything in Cambodia. I bartered them for corn or anything else people would give me, like aspirin, salt, or sugar. For the first few months after the Khmer Rouge took over you could still barter secretly. Things were not as strict and well-organized as they were later. Gradually, the constrictor tightened around us and bartering was extremely dangerous.

As a principal's wife, I had previously had some status and prestige. Some people recognized me, and now that I was ragged and hungry and very thin from the diarrhea that plagued me, some of them even mocked me. I remember one time I had taken lily flowers into the village to try to sell for food for my family. I heard people laugh and point at me and say, "Now look at her." We knew that our situation was precarious because people were acquainted with the fact that Mac was educated. Primary teachers were sometimes spared, but principals and intelligence officers were definitely Khmer Rouge targets.

At the time, Mac's younger brother and his wife and baby lived with us. My sister-in-law had been a soldier in Lon Nol's army. She continually stole fruits and vegetables, and I was constantly worried that she would be caught and our whole family implicated. She became very angry when we tried to caution her. She told me to "mind your own business!" Finally, she convinced her husband that they should strike out on their own and not stay with us. We never were able to find out what happened to them. They just disappeared.

At one point Mac was stricken with diarrhea that was so bad he almost died. You had to report to your supervisor if you did not go to the fields to work for any reason. When the chief of the village heard that Mac was very sick, he took him to a Khmer Rouge hospital. Mac stayed there for a week; he was that sick! The chief of the village saved his life and never told the Khmer Rouge that Mac had been the school principal.

Many years later, when we returned to Cambodia for a visit, we visited a temple near the village where we had first lived as newlyweds and where Mac had been the school principal. The car we were riding in got stuck in the mud. As we waited for assistance, a woman approached us. She was the chief of the village's wife, and he was still alive. We went to see him, and he told us of the fate of those who had worked in Mac's school. Every teacher except one had been killed by the Khmer Rouge. Most had nails driven into their scalps until they expired.

One morning at 9:00 a.m., the head of the village came for Mac and ordered him to follow him. We thought that might be the end of the road for us. Even though I am physically tiny, I was always bold, and I followed them, sneaking from tree to tree so they wouldn't see me. I saw that most of the men of the village were ordered to sit in a circle. But it was simply to communicate what would happen next to them and their families. They were told that they would all have to leave the village and be transported to another place. I was so relieved that Mac would not be killed. But I did know that we would have to prepare for another move. I ran home and told my family to kill all the chickens and pack. Previously, I had gone at night into the village and traded rice, corn, and tobacco for two bikes. I packed the chicken and hid our valuable things, like the medicine, under corn. When Mac came home, he said, "We have to leave." I just said, "We are ready."

CHAPTER SEVEN

DEPORTATION

Mac

I often think about being told we had to leave the village to be transported north. The head of the village simply said, "Angkar needs you." But in reality, he knew that if I stayed in the village where everyone knew me, I would very likely be killed. Now when Simone and I go to Cambodia, we stop and see him. He tells us that he moved us on purpose because he knew that the Khmer Rouge would eventually come and take us away, and we would never be seen again.

It is impossible to describe the sense of dread that became a constant in my life. I never knew if someone approaching me intended to kill me or turn me over to the Khmer Rouge. I never knew if I would be betrayed by a former student, or if somehow a word would slip from my mouth that would give me away. Simone had to be completely silent about my former life. She couldn't gossip with anyone about how we had lived, where we had lived, or who we really were. A false word could be my death warrant. I was not just afraid for myself; I was positive that if I were to be disappeared or murdered, my entire family would also not survive.

Consequently, I was "invisible" for three years, eight months, and twenty days. 3—8—20. I lived on the edge of humanity, silently, turning my face away, looking down, uneducated, pretending I was a simple farmer or fisherman. It was a deadly game and one that took its toll.

To this day, I am subject to night terrors. I wake up screaming, thrashing, and fighting off ghosts of the Khmer Rouge coming to take me from my family. These memories and fears will never be erased from my mind. I have learned to live with them during the day, but at night they come to haunt me.

Simone

We were crowded onto military trucks to leave the village. But as we lined up to be herded onto the trucks, there was a very frightening incident. Khmer Rouge soldiers were checking the things we were carrying. Mac's sister was very intelligent and always carried a book with her. It was disguised, a radio and the book were hidden in a rice bag, and we poured corn on top of them. The soldier was suspicious, and he pulled the radio out of the bag. Then he pulled out the book. But inside the book, she had hidden a photograph of Mac from when he was at the army university in Viet Nam. He immediately yelled at her, "Whose picture is this? Who is in this picture?"

My sister-in-law was so frightened that she could not speak. I could see Mac on the edge of the crowd; he was always trying to be as inconspicuous as possible. I blinked my eyes to communicate with him that there was trouble and he should go away. That was neither the first nor the last time we communicated silently with only our eyes. He turned and walked silently down to the river, away from the lines of people. Then I said to the soldier, "That was my sister's fiancé. Of course, he isn't her fiancé anymore!" The soldier looked closely at the photo and then at my sister-in-law. "Is that right?" he yelled. She nodded *yes* with tears in her eyes, and he took the book and the photo, never to be seen again. That sister did survive the genocide. She lives in Sacramento now. That was an extremely close call. Mac was there in the photo as a lieutenant in the army. He would definitely have been killed immediately if he had been recognized.

We were transported by truck to Krong Pursat, about 150 kilometers northwest of Phnom Penh on National Road 5. After we were unloaded from the military trucks, we waited for two days with no food, no roof over our heads, and no help, until we were herded onto trains. There were no seats and barely room to do anything but stand. Some people tried to squat, but it was insufferably hot and crowded. In our car, we met a family of three—a husband, wife, and their son, who was a university student in Phnom Penh. The lady was older, and terribly ill. Her legs were extremely swollen. There was a lot of fighting, pushing, yelling, and screaming. Everyone was clawing for space and air. Mac and I knew that if we didn't protect her she would be crushed, so I formed a bridge over her with my body.

People were dying everywhere on that train. You had to sleep, urinate, and have bowel movements or diarrhea right where you were. The train never stopped, and there was nothing to eat or drink except what you had managed to hide and bring with you. People were screaming for water and space. Eventually, we reached our destination, and everyone got off. The car was littered with corpses and some of them fell out onto the ground. We were still alive! We invited the old lady and man and their son to find a spot with us to stay together. We all just slept on the ground, exhausted and awaiting our fate.

Mac

Although we initially left Phnom Penh to the south, eventually we were moved to the north and center of the country by truck and train. I had no idea where my parents had gone, but I heard they had been evacuated from the city to the north. I did not expect to ever see them again, and I certainly could not go and search for them. You

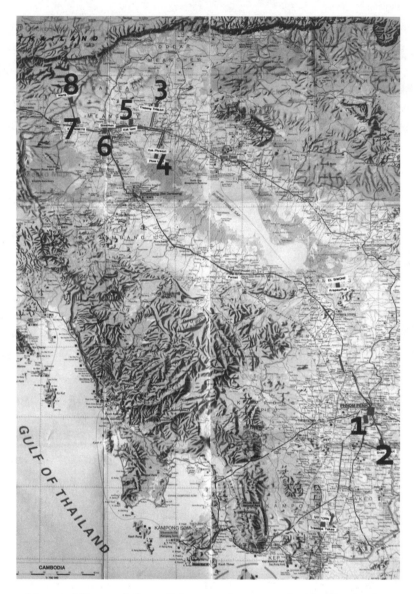

Mac and Simone's forced deportation route inside Cambodia

probably can't understand how devastating this was for a Cambodian. Family ties and respect for parents is incredibly important in our culture. Even though I am now more than seventy years old, I still remember clearly what it felt like to be driven from the city, driven from our home, far from everything familiar, and separated from my parents.

I still love the rain, because back then it meant that there would be crickets and toads to grab and eat. Right from the start, starvation became an issue for all the displaced people. There was nothing to eat, and our family and many others were literally starving. At first the rain meant food. We would eat anything that jumped or crawled but had to be careful not to be caught. If any of us would have been caught, we would be punished or killed. Later, there were no crickets and toads. They had all been eaten by starving people. After the Khmer Rouge came to power, when everyone was forced into labor camps, we would consume anything we could find—lizards, frogs, snakes. We would even eat red ants. Those ants would build nests in the trees. We would place a vessel with water underneath and tap on the nest until the ants fell out. Once they landed in the water they would emit some kind of fluid. We would then boil the water with the ants in it and eat it.

One time we even resorted to eating papaya bark. I can't describe how bitter it is. Simone swam across a river to retrieve that bark, and she had never really learned how to swim. She dragged a few branches across the currents to save us. We were that desperate. We would spear rats that lived in the trees during the rainy season and in holes in the ground during the dry season. We had no true weapons, so we fashioned spears from bamboo. When you got a rat, you felt as if you had achieved something special. Protein for your children!

People died everywhere. Animals died too. People don't think of that. They didn't have enough to eat either, or they were eaten themselves. And there were diseases and no medications for diarrhea and malaria. At night, you would hear wolves. People also don't know that there are wolves in Cambodia. They would howl, and if a person was too weak, he was fair game for the wolves.

As I told you, Cambodians had many superstitions. For example, many believed that if you heard an owl at night, someone was going to die. It was said that the spirits sent birds to pick up the dead people. That's what the elders would say. I remember the unearthly sound of the birds screaming at night under the Khmer Rouge. The birds must have been very busy because there were dead everywhere.

I believe that the strict control of food and the restrictions on when, where, and what you were allowed to eat were more than just part of the Maoist ideology. It was a very efficient means of controlling the population. When you are 100% dependent on Angkar for the food you need for yourself and your family, you are unlikely to rebel. In fact, you are too weak to rebel. This was more important to the regime than the development of a strong labor force. They did not care who lived and died. They desired complete control, eliminating all potential of disobedience and disloyalty to Angkar.

When the Khmer Rouge ruled, they had an army that controlled regions through village people that they recruited. Village people had no choice but to comply with the Khmer Rouge, or they themselves would be killed. Some believed in the Khmer Rouge ideology, but many were themselves simply trying to survive. People from the cities were moved all over the country. At the time, there didn't seem to be any rhyme or reason. Now I understand that the transports were designed to prevent community loyalties or bases of power that might challenge the Khmer Rouge. People were not moved simply to provide labor. There were more complex motives.

But to me, it was important to move away from towns where I was known. A school principal is known by many people. Not that many people knew of my work as an army intelligence officer, but

I had many former students and teachers who knew me. If anyone had pointed me out to the Khmer Rouge, I would be a dead man. We were remarkably fortunate that none of our former teachers, students, or parents of students gave us away. I had always tried to be a fair man and a good principal, and Simone was beloved in our village. She always helped everyone, and I believe that is why no one betrayed us. As for me, I kept my head down, tried not to draw any attention to myself, and pretended I didn't understand the simplest things. To survive, I kept silent and cooperated. I couldn't show that I was anything but an uneducated farmer or a fisherman. When we were moved north by the town leader, our lives were probably saved.

We lived in ignorance about who was issuing orders. The Khmer Rouge had divided the country into five regions. Each region was governed slightly differently—some more harshly, some a little more leniently. Region 5, where we eventually lived in the north, was very tough. Work was incredibly hard. We proved our value to Angkar through appearing to work vigorously at whatever task was given to us. People were punished and tortured if they were too weak to perform the way the Khmer Rouge wanted—but really, the population was considered expendable.

Just as each region had slightly different rules and cultures, the whole country underwent a transition from disorganized in terms of what was expected to complete control. At first, families were allowed to eat with each other and maybe even pick some vegetables and fruits. However, later on, as the noose tightened, no one was allowed to eat individually. No one was allowed to possess or grow any food of their own. You and your family all went to one main dining area at the same time and were fed a small portion from a common pot. You took a terrible risk if you hid food. There was no such thing as privacy. If you were caught, you would simply disappear. There was no jail or detention per se that I know of, except in Phnom Penh. If the Khmer Rouge chose to eliminate you, one night, after dark, there would be some soldiers at your door who would say, "Angkar needs you." And you would go with them and never be seen again. When the communal eating started, the Khmer Rouge never ate with us, but we suspected that they were well-fed. They never looked hungry. We only received watery rice porridge, and very little of that, usually once a day. Everyone had to work, even small children. And wives, too, unless they were caring for a very young infant. Later on, after we moved to the north part of the country, Simone worked in the fields while I fished. The labor was backbreaking from sun up to sunset. Hard labor like that requires energy, but we had no fuel for our bodies. If you failed to work hard, you would be whipped, or you would disappear. Or you would simply die from starvation and disease. Some people just gave up.

The reality was that I had a family, and they were starving. I had a wife, three children, later a baby, and eventually—when we were unexpectedly reunited—my mother and father, who were old and frail. One of my children, Mara, was often sick. In the north, I worked as a fisherman. I will tell you soon how that came to be— I, who was a school principal and army intelligence officer. Every day I would go and fish with two other men. Cambodia has an abundance of fish in several very large lakes. I could catch fish, crab, eels, snakes—anything to kill and bring back with me. The fish were to supply the Khmer Rouge soldiers and the communal cafeteria. During the monsoon season, fish were especially abundant. I could hide a fish in the bushes and sneak out in the dark, when I thought I wouldn't be seen, to retrieve it. When I couldn't find it again, I would be devastated. But I got really good at remembering where a fish was hidden. This was strictly forbidden. If caught, I would have disappeared. There were spies and informants everywhere. Sometimes they hid in the branches of trees. Even young children had been brainwashed and "turned" by the Khmer Rouge. I was terrified of getting caught, because if I were killed, six other members of my family would have perished also. Therefore, I was very careful.

Living in America, it is hard to visualize the total darkness of the Cambodian nights during those years. There was absolutely no illumination at night except sometimes the moon and stars. Most nights it was black and therefore easy to be invisible if you could be silent. Black like the clothes the Khmer Rouge wore. Black like the evil that had descended upon the innocent Cambodian people.

Simone

When we were evacuated from Phnom Penh, we went one way and my parents (my mother and stepfather) went another. They disappeared during the genocide and I never saw them again. I never found out what happened to them or where and when they died. It was impossible to go in search of our families. We had to go where we were told to go. There was no information about anything—no newspapers or radios or TVs. Any news we ever received of family and friends was simply word of mouth. And we had to be very careful about talking, because we never knew who was listening and who would make us an item of suspicion. I rarely talked to anyone, even my husband. Our conversations were very limited and confined to simple things. We instinctively knew that communication was dangerous. There were not only pineapple eyes everywhere; there were listeners, even if we didn't know where they lurked.

Mac

After the horrendous train ride, we were unloaded at Svay Sisophon, about 250 kilometers northwest of Phnom Penh, at the junction of National Road #5 and #6. I remember it was the middle of the night—very dark. We were simply dumped by the side of the tracks with no shelter or food. The next day we were crowded onto military trucks to continue our journey. We had absolutely no idea where we were going, and of course, one never asked questions like that. We were simply part of a faceless group of ragged, weak, hungry people, afraid for our lives and the lives of our loved ones.

I was at the very back of an open truck absolutely packed with people. The truck was crowded, the roads were pitted and treacherous, and the branches were low-slung. About five kilometers north of Svay Sisophon, on Road #6, there was a checkpoint near a bridge. The checkpoint had a pole that served as a gate. I was struck with this pole as the truck pulled away and was thrown off the truck onto the road. I knew I was severely injured because of the extreme pain. In fact, I had broken my hip. They stopped and picked me up and put me back on a truck. The pain was excruciating. At the temple, we all disembarked and were told that Angkar would come and pick us up. Soon cow wagons appeared, and we were transported by villagers into the village. For six months, I could not work at hard labor. I walked crooked and had constant pain. Eventually I healed somewhat. Obviously, I wasn't much use to the Khmer Rouge. I thought it was only a matter of time before they would decide that my life was no longer worth anything to Angkar and soldiers would appear at my door at night.

Mia

During one of our "transports," we were in a big army truck packed with other people/families. There was hardly any room to move. We came to a check point where they had a booth with a long wooden board/arm that would go up and down. Because of the way we were crammed into the truck, my dad was standing up to make room for an old woman to sit down. When we passed thru the check point, the board must have come down too quickly without my dad seeing it, and he was knocked off the truck. He got hurt but he was smart enough to put his arms up to protect his head. They took him away in a separate truck to have him looked at but did not tell us where they were taking him. My mom and Mara were both crying. Mom was terribly worried that they were going to take him away and kill him.

They took us to this open field in the middle of nowhere. No trees or bushes, just flat land. It was pouring rain and the wind was cold. Mom used some sort of bedsheet to put over us but it leaked; we had no way to stay dry. I don't know why I remember that cold and miserable night so vividly.

CHAPTER EIGHT

CATERPILLAR VILLAGE

Mac

When they took us to the village, it was already dark. Simone and I tried to be friendly with the driver of the cart that picked us up, as we did with everyone. That is probably another secret of our survival. People responded to our friendliness. We asked him if we would find food in the village, and he said yes, there were cocoons to eat. Then he took us to his own home where his wife fed us a little bit of porridge and a cocoon!

Simone

I remember that kindness very well. He fed us not only porridge, but also a cocoon. At that time in that place, communal eating had not yet been ordered. That cocoon tasted pretty good! We lived for about six months in that village and soon learned that every house in the village had been ordered to make silk. Mac was unable to do hard labor because of his hip, but he was put to work making long bamboo trays to be used in the silk production. My job was to feed the caterpillars. I had to pick leaves in the countryside and take them in to feed the caterpillars that then produced silk.

The old woman from the train died in the caterpillar village. Their son never forgot that we had helped her. Mac helped bury her, a very important thing to do in our culture. As we were eventually trying to flee Cambodia, in the chaos when people finally possessed some food and animals if they could find them, he gave us a cow. We ate that cow and it probably saved us. By then we were all so malnourished and weak that it would take a long time for each of us to recover. How grateful we were for the sustenance of that cow. We thanked the boy from the bottom of our hearts. Later, that boy stepped on a mine, and it killed him. The mine was almost exactly in the spot where Mac had fallen off the tuck and broken his hip. There is a thin line between life and death, luck and tragedy.

One of my brothers-in-law and his wife were still alive at that time, and they lived nearby. He had married a woman who had been a female soldier in Lon Nol's army. She stole many things, a lot of the time, and was always trying to find out what had happened to her parents. No one really knew how the Khmer Rouge found out that she was stealing, or perhaps about her former life. She did talk a lot; and in Pol Pot's Cambodia, only the silent could survive. One day the Khmer Rouge came to her hut and killed her, my brother-in-law, and their son. Just like that—no explanations, no mercy.

In that village, we did not live with the first farmer who helped us by feeding us the porridge and the cocoon. He was not allowed to keep us. We were placed with a different Original family. I had never seen such poor people. Their clothes were rags and they slept on filthy mats. Their dishes were dented and they ate with their fingers, not spoons.

At one point the woman of the house became very ill, as did one of her children. I went to her and offered to help. She agreed, and I was able to give her and the child some of the medicine I had brought from Phnom Penh. They recovered, and she became my friend. Nevertheless, we had practically no food to eat, and it was apparent that my children were starving and malnourished. One day the grandmother of the house beckoned me to follow her into the yard. There she gave me a small shovel and told me to dig. I had no idea what I was digging for. I doubted this poor family had hidden jewels or gold. Eventually my shovel hit a big pot. In the pot was sweet rice that the grandmother had hidden in case the family ever needed it. She gave me a portion to help me feed my family.

I believe deeply that our parents' spirits watch over us when they die. I believe deeply that we need to live with kindness and generosity. My husband and I both always tried to help others in need. We believed in befriending people. That was our philosophy of life, but it also aided greatly in the survival of our family. Just as we helped others, sometimes people helped us. I believe that when we returned after the evacuation to the village where my husband had been the principal, we were never betrayed because people respected us. We had always tried to be good and fair friends. We were not betrayed, even though most of my husband's former students had joined the Khmer Rouge.

We were still terribly worried about our families. There was a cow wagon trail that I walked on to go to work. Every day there were many caravans of cow wagons. I would always ask, "Where are you from; where are you going?" One day, as more wagons were passing through the village, I asked where they were from. Someone said Takeo—I repeated the word—and heard Mac's cousin cry out. She recognized my voice. She shouted, "We're here; we're here." A miracle happened during that time. I couldn't believe my eyes. There were Mac's mom and dad on one of the wagons. I ran up to the Khmer army soldier guarding the group and pleaded with him to let me take them all with me. I said, "I am their daughter and they are too old. They will die on this march. Let me take them and care for them." But he wouldn't let them stay with me.

I raced home and told Mac the amazing story that his parents were on a march in a wagon, headed for a temple, but that the soldiers would not allow me to take them. Mac, even though he was severely crippled, went as fast as he could to the temple and spoke very politely to the soldiers. He told them he worked for Angkar as a farmer. The soldier finally let him take his parents, but they would not let the cousin go with us. Mac's parents surely would have died if we had not found them and intervened. After that, they lived with us. We were now responsible for a lot of our family.

The village was called Phum Poy Char, and it was located near Trapeang Thmar Lake. The family we lived with was named Sar Ngoch. By that time, we were dressed all in black. Our clothes were given to us by the Khmer Rouge. No one was allowed to wear any colors. We went to work at dawn and came home at dusk. We were given a small amount of rice porridge to eat every evening. At that time, everything was about the food we tried to find to eat. There was no way a family could survive on the small amount of rice we were given. We ate everything we could find—roots, bark, flowers, insects, toads. Hunger is a terrible thing.

Mac

Cambodia had been turned back to the stone age. It was the Year Zero. Tools and technology were primitive or nonexistent. There was no way to communicate. Yet every morning from dawn to dusk in the villages a loudspeaker would blare Khmer Rouge songs and propaganda. The songs were about the evil American imperialists and the glory of the Khmer Rouge. They were very loud—you could not escape them. I was extremely curious about how those loudspeakers worked—with no electricity apparent. One day I decided to find out. On some excuse, I climbed a little ladder to look into the tiny hut from which the noise was emanating. There were two skinny Cambodians turning a makeshift bicycle wheel to generate power. All day long! The music blared, "Kill the American Imperialists."

Simone

We were often sick. We had no shoes and our feet were full of scabs and foot rot. Many people lost their teeth. There was no way to keep clean—no soap. We washed in rivers or lakes that were polluted with decaying corpses. It became so common to see them that our children didn't even comment on them anymore. We lost all or most of our hair. Our bodies were just bones covered with bruised skin. We were covered with lice all over our scalps and even in our eyebrows. We went to sleep every night wondering if we would awaken to see the dawn and wondering if our children would make it through another day.

CHAPTER NINE

TAKEN AWAY

Mac

The day the Khmer Rouge came to take me away was one of the lowest moments of my life. They came for me at dusk, as they usually did. Men in typical Khmer Rouge uniforms would come to a family unexpectedly. They usually did not brandish guns. They had knives and spoke nicely. "Comrade, friend, Angkar needs you. You must come with us and not take anything with you." There were two young Khmer Rouge soldiers, and I did not know them.

I was absolutely sure that I would never come back. I needed to say goodbye to my parents and to Simone. In the United States, you would hug your parents; but in the Buddhist tradition, you bow completely to the ground to show deep respect. I bowed in this way three times to them. I asked a blessing for them. I was convinced that this was the last time I would see my wife, my children, and my parents. There was a deep sadness and resignation within me. And hopelessness, too. I did not hug Simone. We did not speak. I just looked at her and she looked at me with a gaze that spoke more than words. A gaze of finality, resignation, and unfathomable sadness.

Simone

Whenever any man was taken away, a wife could simply assume she would now be a widow. No one ever came back. In my heart, I believed that this was the end of our entire family. I knew I could not keep everyone alive without my husband. I fell into deep mourning for the loss of Mac, and also in anticipation of the other losses that I felt sure would be our destiny.

Mac

I was not tied up at that time. The guards pointed in one direction and I walked between them. I turned around many times to see my family—and then one last time. Finally, I turned a corner and could see them no more.

As the Khmer Rouge marched me away, we joined a group of many men from the village. We walked for about ten miles, completely silent, and afraid to speak to each other. I didn't know these men. We just walked quietly until sundown, finally encountering a big Buddhist temple at a place I now know was Phum Srok. Each one of us was tied against the wall, hands behind us, inside the temple. At one point one hand was freed and we were given a little rice porridge to eat. Nobody said anything inside that temple. It was pitch black and completely silent. Sadness lingered over us like a low mist. When the Khmer Rouge picked you up, you could expect to be killed.

We were left there until morning. If we had to go to the toilet, three people had to go together guarded by a soldier with an AK47. There were probably a couple hundred men in that temple. In the morning light, I could see that there were many more than I had thought.

We were probably about 30 or 40 kilometers from the Thai border, and I thought about trying to escape, if my hands were ever untied. But how could you escape? We were heavily guarded, and we had no food. We didn't know where we were. Finally, the door opened, guards entered, and we were given a handful of rice. Then the doors were closed again.

Eventually, when it was fully light, the door opened again. There was a meeting in a courtyard under a tree with a man speaking into a microphone. He said that Angkar needed specialists to rebuild the country. He told us to tell the truth about our skills, and we could rebuild the country together. We were given a paper with a few questions on it. We were told that if we lied we would be killed. They were simple questions like, "Where are you from?" "What did you do before the Khmer Rouge came to power?" "Who are your parents?" "Are you married?" "Who are your friends?" Because I had been to intelligence school, I knew this tactic. I needed to remember exactly what I said each time in order that I wouldn't be inconsistent and caught in a lie. They gave that paper to us three different times. I always gave the simplest of answers. The simpler, the better. If I would have put in details, I could have forgotten what I had said.

Some of the captives were excited! Perhaps they could go back to their former professions. Some even falsified their answers to seem useful to Angkar. "Artillery, head of police, professor…" Those people were condemning themselves to certain execution.

At that time, the Khmer Rouge divided people into those who had been brought into the region and those who had been born in the villages in the region. They were very suspicious of those who had been transported in. All those transported in lived with or among villagers, who observed us carefully. Some were recruited to spy on us. Therefore, to stay safe you had to be as invisible and silent as possible. Say little, divulge nothing of your former life, and act as if you are a simple person who is friendly but not very intelligent. A good laborer. That's how you might survive.

On the fourth day, there was no meeting in the morning. In late afternoon, two military trucks arrived, and men were called to be taken away by those trucks, about thirty per truck. Some were called by name to be transported and executed. The next day, the two trucks returned and collected more men. I was in the last group to be collected, and about twenty men remained to be picked up. A covered truck arrived in the dark that evening and we were all loaded into it. I was extremely frightened. It was dark, the truck was covered, and no one could see what would happen to us. We traveled for about three or four hours—from the temple to a main road—probably traveling East on Road # 6 for two hours, and then off the main road. Finally, the truck stopped, the back gate was dropped, and we were told to get out, sit down, and stay there. By that time it was absolutely pitch dark. We were not tied, but we had no idea of where we were. We couldn't even see the stars because we were under a canopy of trees. None of us could sleep with the fear of what would happen to us. It was probably around midnight, and we could see nothing. There were no lights anywhere. That is one of my most persistent memories of my time under the Khmer Rouge. Ignorance and darkness. No light. I guess there is a parallel. There was no escape; we were lost in the dark. But as light filtered through the branches with the dawn, I heard a rooster, and for some reason its call gave me hope. I had survived another night and there was life somewhere.

Guards came to us. They were probably only twelve to fifteen years old and they carried AK-47s. They told us we would be following a wagon trail and heading south. Everyone got up and stood in a line. There were perhaps thirty people in that line, and I was about five back from the front. The guards didn't want you to see them. They walked behind us or far to the side. The sun rose, and I could see more clearly. I turned around a lot and saw that the line was getting shorter and shorter. Men were disappearing. As we walked I tried to move up in the line because men were disappearing from the back. On and on we marched, from dawn until about 3:00 p.m.

When we stopped, there were only three men left, and I was the third. Everyone else was gone. I didn't know where or how it had happened, but I assumed the worst. We stopped at a little hut near a jungle and a big lake. There were trees and high water. The hut was probably for farmers to have some shelter as they collected rice. The guards left and told us to stay with an old, illiterate jungle man who was sitting in the hut. He looked very strong and dark. Although the man was frightening, I went and sat next to him and talked politely. Surprisingly, he gave us a little bit of rice and salt and a small pan. I called him Daddy, a term of respect, and asked him if he would let me try to catch some fish and shrimp. He said yes, and we ate for the first time in several days.

One of the three of us had been with the state police, and one was a mechanic who worked with helicopters. At first all three of us stayed at the hut with the old man, and I was able to take them to fish with me once I started to fish. Eventually the guards came back and took the other two men away. One of them died in the genocide; the other one managed to survive. The old man protected us and saved us as long as he could. Though people were frightened by the Khmer Rouge, many whom I encountered were human enough to show me kindness.

Fear of his appearance had almost kept me from engaging with the old jungle man. I believe this is another lesson from my journey through the genocide. Respect one another; help one another. Simply sitting down and talking with the forbidding old man that day helped save our lives.

I stayed with the old man and eventually saw two men, original villagers, who were fishing. I asked if I could go with them, and the old man said *yes*. I talked with the two fishermen and offered to carry all of their things for them. I also had ideas about how to fish. The two men decided that they wanted to take a nap; and while they napped, I fished. When they woke up, fish had been caught! I guess they saw that I could be useful, so from that time on, I became a fisherman too. The two fishermen were happy to have me with them. I worked very hard, caught lots of fish, and carried all their things. I was always nervous though. I lived with the fear that I would be picked up any minute. A school principal, an army intelligence officer, and now a fisherman!

One day, as I was heading back to the hut after fishing, I saw four black figures in the distance coming my way. At first I wasn't sure what the figures were, but I had a sinking feeling in my stomach. As they came closer and I continued to walk toward them, I saw that they were four Khmer Rouge soldiers. I felt they must be coming to take me away. I must have been found out. They were real soldiers and not kids like many of the Khmer Rouge. They had come to the old jungle man's hut to find fish to eat, and they talked to him about the catch. When they saw me, they said, "Comrade, come in and eat!" I tried to act calm and ignorant as I grilled fish for them. Although they stared at me continually and came to eat several times after that day, they never questioned me, except about fishing. I had quickly picked up the local dialect, and my skin was now very dark from the sun. I wore tattered clothes, never brushed my teeth, and was constantly dirty. Blending in, becoming invisible, and losing my former identity was the only way to survive.

The rainy season in Cambodia is in August and September. I stayed in the hut during the dry season, but upon the onset of the rains, I went back to a village to live because one couldn't live in the hut; it was under five feet of water.

At some point, the two men I fished with took me to another little village. They said it was for one day. Astonishingly, when I got there, Simone and my family had been brought to me. I had no idea how this happened. My dad, mom, children and Simone had been brought in a cow wagon from about 60 kilometers away. This was extremely unusual—the reuniting of a family. Even families belonged to Angkar. We never really found out why we were reunited.

Somebody must have been watching out for my family. The Khmer Rouge generally believed in separating families. They did not allow hugging and kissing; they thought it was bad for the discipline of the country. But someone must have taken pity on Simone and our struggles. When we were reunited, I showed no emotion. I simply bowed with respect to my parents.

The new village was called Wat Tonn Lapp and was located along the Tapon River, about 40 kilometers south of Road #6. In this village, there was only communal eating. It was in a region that was strictly run. We planted corn, tomatoes, eggplant, and chilies, but only for Angkar's use. We were forbidden to hide any of the vegetables for use by our families. I stayed there only one night, and then went back to the fishing hut. Subsequently, I visited the village often; on one of those visits, Simone became pregnant.

Simone

When Mac was taken away, I was terrified and depressed. I tried to work extremely hard, but I was light-skinned and looked like a city person. I did not blend well. Some people didn't seem to like me; others did like me. We lived with an older man, and he found out that I knew how to sew. Soon I was working in the fields but also sewing in a house with three other ladies. This house was next to a small "school." At that time, schools were very primitive. Young children gathered under a tree, learned Khmer Rouge propaganda, and sang Khmer Rouge songs. One of the teachers there thought I was a widow. I sensed that he had a "crush" on me. He came every day and sat on a stool next to me and watched me sew. He wanted to marry me, but I told him that I did not know for sure that my husband was dead, and that perhaps he would come back! I felt sorry for him but I said, "I cannot marry you." Nevertheless, the teacher gave us some fish and palm sugar. He was attached to the Khmer Rouge and dressed all in black. One day he told me to get ready to leave the village. The leader of the village also told me to pack. Some of the family was piled onto an ox wagon, and some of us walked. I had no idea where we were going or why. I thought we all might be killed.

We left around ten in the morning and walked all day. My little brother was with me, and my two sisters-in-law who were only teenagers. They were eventually sent to work on dam construction where one died of starvation. Lots of young people died there. The older sister was the one who survived the genocide and now lives in California. When we were told to stop, the guards said, "Here is your spot. Make a hut!" My little brother really helped with that hut. By this time, I was very weak and truly needed that help. We were given a knife with which to cut bamboo and palm leaves. We made a little hut together. Later, my little brother died near one of the temples.

All of a sudden I saw someone approaching from far away. It looked like my husband, but at first I dismissed that thought. It could not be Mac. I had accepted that he was most likely gone from us forever. This person approaching was very dark and dirty. I guess I was in shock when I saw it was really Mac. We did not hug, nor did we talk. No one asked the other how he had survived. Mac simply bowed deeply to his parents, and our eyes met, conveying fidelity, pain, love, and relief. Mac left the next day, and then came back and forth on an irregular basis. I have often wondered whether the teacher who loved me arranged the reunion of our family with Mac. It will forever remain a mystery.

My new job was to take excrement out to a field where it would be dried and used as fertilizer for the rice fields. I didn't complain; I just did as I was told. You had to act as if you loved your work. I looked like a skeleton, but I still showed them that I loved Angkar and was devoted to laboring for Angkar. I was so skinny that my mother-in-law said that my breasts looked like raisins. I was completely flat. While I labored, my mother-in-law took care of the children; and I watered plants, shoveled excrement, and flipped earth with a hoe.

There were no schools as we now think of them. Children were gathered under a tree to talk about Angkar. They were told that Angkar would take care of them, and that the parents' job was done.

The Khmer Rouge used children even against their own parents. Even though my children were very young, they already worked for Angkar at various tasks, like gathering and stacking wood.

Brutality was everywhere. I remember the constant fear that we would be killed. It fostered extreme hyper-vigilance. We were always on our guard, but at the same time, we could not appear too frightened or we would attract suspicion. And we always were driven to search for food. We ate everything we could find. We were allowed to catch and eat snakes, but we also ate grass roots, centipedes, toads, and crickets. We foraged for the roots of the banana tree, and all vermin were fair game. A little mouse was valuable protein. Mac talks about the sweet sounds of crickets and toads after the rains in Cambodia. But they were silenced during the genocide. They had all been consumed.

CHAPTER TEN

NEW VILLAGE, NEW BABY

Mia

At some point we were taken to a village where people had already been situated before we arrived. We got only one scoop of porridge a day. The porridge ingredients consisted of a few pieces of rice and water. I remember every day being hungry, very hungry. I witnessed a lot of people being physically abused just because they were hungry and asked for more porridge. If they didn't do what they told them to do, they'd hit them with a whip, push them on the ground, and kick them with their feet. The ones who were too sick to work were left to starve to death. Inhumane living conditions—indescribable! We didn't have shoes, clothes, or even toilet paper to wipe ourselves with. To relieve ourselves we would go either behind our place or to an open field and use sticks or leaves. We ate with our hands and drank from a bowl. When it was dry and there was no rain, we had to drink from the same river that the dead bodies were floating down. The water was very contaminated.

When my father was returned to us, he would dig a little hole near by the water and use that as a filter for us to drink. We were all so skinny from malnutrition. For some reason, I was the only one whose hands and feet weren't swollen. We lived on insects and anything we could find to eat we ate. We ate banana roots, grass roots, and any kind of leaves that looked edible. I don't remember worrying too much about whether or not the leaves and roots were poisonous. Maybe we were just lucky or we figured we were going to die sooner or later anyway so what was the difference. My father was a fisherman for the Khmer Rouge. Sometimes he'd secretly bring some fish home to us. If he had been caught doing that, they would have killed him.

There were a lot of Cambodians that died due to starvation. I remember seeing many dead bodies/rotting human corpses out in the open fields as I went looking for food.

Mac

I fished with two men. They had told me confidentially about their past lives; one had been an airplane mechanic and the other a police officer. I never told them that I had been an Army intelligence officer. One day, as I was sitting with them in the village, three young Khmer Rouge soldiers approached. They stood in front of us and said to the two men, "Comrades, come with us. Angkar needs you." The soldiers did not choose me. I never knew why. One of the fishermen was killed, but the other appeared again in our lives, at a time when food was almost nonexistent during the floods. Nevertheless, Simone took pity and shared a potato with him. Her heart would not allow her to see someone suffer.

After the two men were taken, my responsibilities were almost unbearable. I was given a long canoe and a net, and I had to find fish for Angkar and for the whole village. I was given one helper. One day, when the water was retreating, we needed to row towards the jungle to find fish that had retreated with the water. Many groups from different villages had also come there to fish, and that night they settled in the jungle to sleep. I was always on guard. We slept in the canoe and did not join the group. In the middle of the night, we heard gunfire. Everyone sleeping there had been ambushed and killed. When we returned to the village, I reported the ambush to the chief of the village. He did not say anything at all. I think he knew.

Sometimes the fish were not biting. On one occasion, the rains were torrential. I knew I could not catch fish while it was raining like that, so I waited until the rain stopped when the fish could be caught. As darkness fell, I kept on fishing. There was a curfew in effect. Anyone caught outside after sunset could be immediately stopped and "arrested." As I entered the village after dark with my fish and my fishing gear, two young Khmer Rouge soldiers appeared in front of me and said, "Comrade, put down your fish. We are going to tie you up." They were very polite! They tied my hands behind my back with a rope and walked about 45 minutes with me to a big mango tree. They tied my hands and legs to that tree and left me there. I was certain that they would kill me. All I could think about was that my family would not survive without me. They wouldn't have any idea that I had been taken. I was deeply sad inside, and thought that these were my last minutes on earth.

There was no escaping the ropes with which I was tied. Mosquitos nearly ate me alive as I stayed tied to the mango tree. Eventually, after dark, the soldiers returned with several more Khmer Rouge. I could hear them walking toward me on dead leaves. They had flashlights and pointed them at me, going up and down my body. I recognized some as the ones that had eaten the fish I had grilled in the old man's hut. They looked and looked at me and discussed my fate. I could hear them say, "He is not the one. Let him go."

Miraculously, they finally cut the rope from my wrist and legs, gave me a little food, and escorted me home. They told me to speak of this experience to absolutely no one. I never told Simone what had happened until we were in the United States. And she never asked. There were things you just didn't talk about.

No one could really be trusted. You could never let down your guard. I remember a young man who had been married by Angkar to a young woman. He constantly stole food for his wife. She betrayed the very man whom she had married and who risked everything by stealing for her. He was told to kneel by the river and was then struck on the back of his head by a young Khmer soldier, falling into the water. Miraculously, he had survived the blows and swam to other side of the river. Then he was apprehended and brought back to the village. That evening, after returning from the cafeteria, we saw him hanging from a tree, killed by the Khmer Rouge, but really murdered by the duplicity of his wife.

Even the village chiefs were not safe. There were rivalries and struggles for power everywhere. The first village chief in the place where we lived before the floods was killed by a rival chief who entered the village, representing a different regional arm of the Khmer Rouge. We heard the man screaming, calling out for his family. "Please help me; please save me." The next day he was gone.

Simone

At that time, my little brother had been taken away to work on a construction project. He was eighteen at the time, and young men were separated from their families at that age and carefully supervised so they would not grow to oppose the regime. He stayed away for quite a long time, and then he was returned to us, with a badly infected leg. It was gangrenous, and I tended to it every day, wiping it with a tamarind leaf, trying to keep it clean. Finally the village chief told me that he would have to go to the "temple." The temple was supposed to be a hospital, but really those who went in never came out. There was no medicine—and even less food than in the village. People were just sent there to die.

I visited my brother every day on my way home from work, bringing him any food I could hide. On the last day that I saw him, he was terribly sick. He said he was dying, but I told him that he was too young to die. He told me to look at his body. His skin from the neck down was raw and seeping from wounds where he had been whipped with a chain and a hose over and over again. Because he was starving, when he found a chicken that had been loose around the temple, he ate it. The man in the bed next to him betrayed him to the guards, and he was punished severely for having taken something that "belonged to Angkar." He died that night.

When I became pregnant, I hardly believed it. The signs were there—I felt sick in the mornings and I craved jackfruit. At dawn, before anyone arose, I would walk to the temple where my little brother had died; there was jackfruit everywhere. I picked up small ones; they were very bitter. Nowadays, experts say that the jackfruit is highly nutritious. My son Jason would also sneak out and bring them to me. I was really nauseated though. I continued to work throughout my pregnancy, and my children helped a lot bringing water and wood to our hut. On one of those occasions, Mia was bitten by a rodent. Then she too became very ill.

When the time came to have the baby, I sent a message to my supervisor that I could not work on the fertilizer. A lady midwife was sent to me. The word for that is like the word for a younger sister. There was no doctor and no sterilization. Just a tray and rusty scissors. This was my banana-root baby who lived for six months, until I could no longer give him milk and he starved to death.

Mia

When my Mother's water broke, we thought she had peed herself. Then she yelled out for my grandma. I'm not sure if my Dad was there or not, but she told us to find someone to help deliver the baby. During her labor, she was screaming really loud; and we got nervous and we (Jason, Mara, and myself) went underneath the house and discovered two medium-size Jars filled with... I think it was brown sugar cane… something like honey. I, being the trouble-maker, saw an opportunity to take advantage of the situation while Mom was in labor. I told Jason and Mara, "If we don't tell Mom about this, she won't know. We'll just eat a little bit, not too much. We were using our fingers to lick it up, but before we knew it half the jar was gone. Grandma came looking for us. She found us but never said anything about what we did. She just told Jason and me to go get some water from the river and gather some wood to put underneath Mom's hard bamboo bed to keep her and the baby warm. Jason and I would make bets along the way; the loser would have to carry the water from the river all the way back home or most of the way anyway. A couple days later, my mom needed some sugar and saw that the jar was half empty. She had us line up and started to interrogate us. Jason and I didn't say anything, but Mara started to cry, and then she pointed at me and I got hit several times.

I was never really afraid to do anything. I climbed the palm trees with Jason, I learned how to swim and float across the river. It was a pretty good-size river. Sometimes the water would be moving pretty fast. One time I got really scared and tired so I just floated on my back. Someone mentioned that the river was haunted because many dead people had been thrown into it. They told me that once I reached the middle of the river if I felt something really cold rushing up my legs that it was the spirits of the dead who would pull me down and drown me. I figured they were just trying to scare me because they didn't want me to go to the other side of the river where the vegetables were because they wanted them for themselves. I wasn't sure if the leaves or vegetables were safe to eat or not, but I was determined to get them and show them to my mom. These kinds of vegetables only grew near the water and were only on the other side of the river; none were on our side. Sometimes when they didn't have me working, picking up rocks to build bridges or walls to block water, or doing something else in the rice fields, I'd dig grass roots. Basically,

I was always looking for food, whether it was small creatures, any kind of insects, edible or not. Then I would bring it back to show my mom to see if we could cook it and share it with my family....

Every evening till midnight I'd hear the Khmer Rouge singing and dancing. I was curious and would sneak out and watch them. I even started to participate in the ceremonies, but then I got caught by my mom one night. She told me I was too young to dance, and that was the end of that.

One day while I was down by the river, I saw a pile of wood. Underneath the wood, I saw what I thought was a big mouse; it turned out to be a rat. To me that was dinner, so I tried to grab it with my bare hands. I got a hold of its tail, but it turned around and bit me, so I let go and it got away. I went home with a bloody finger and told my mom what had happened. I ended up getting really sick from it. I almost died because it had rabies, but by a miracle I survived. I still have a little scar from it on my finger.

Some people ask me if I remember anything about those years in Cambodia. My husband is interested in those times, but most other people have no idea what really happened and what it was like. To them I say, imagine the worst things you can imagine—and it was more awful than that. I remember all the dead bodies—bodies floating in the rivers. They were everywhere.

I also remember the leeches. There were several kinds of leeches; and in the north where we were, the puddles and wet places were full of them. The buffalo leech is black and green with a stripe on its side. They are huge and extremely difficult to remove. You can't eat them; they can make you very sick. They smell your blood and will attach to your body wherever they can.

I remember one incident in particular. It was the rainy season, it was flooded everywhere, and the water was contaminated. I remember my grandma and I tried to walk thru the flood. In places the water was up to my waist, but then again, I was small. I remember seeing floating dead bodies wrapped up like mummies. They were floating all around me. The water was full of leeches also. They were all over the dead bodies; and by the time I got back to the hut, I had a couple of them hanging on my legs; one was by my private parts. I was so scared I started to cry. I thought that I was going to die. There were none on my grandma. I guess they were on me because I had cuts on my legs and ankles that had gotten infected and the leeches had smelled the blood. My grandma was brave; she pulled them off me. To this day, I still sometimes have nightmares about it.

Mac

In addition to laboring in the fields, the Khmer Rouge had many building projects. For example, they decided to build dams across the rivers. The problem was that the Khmer Rouge had no engineering expertise or experience, and no modern building and construction techniques. All the engineers had been exterminated. Everything was constructed with primitive tools and manual labor. These dams were a perfect example of Khmer Rouge insanity. Without dams, during the rainy season the waters from Thailand could move freely into the lakes. But with the dams, and not very sturdy ones, the waters spread into a broad mouth, and then broke through the weak and ill-constructed dams, creating terrible floods.

In this village, Simone eventually was ordered to work on dam construction along with her two sisters. This was terribly hard work, and because it was away from the village and extremely strenuous, it was like a punishment. One of her sisters died there from starvation. How Simone came to work on the dam project is another story of potential danger and death, one in which Simone barely escaped with her life.

Simone

I labored hard in this village. But I always felt uneasy. I was suspect for several reasons. First, I was light skinned and married to a dark-skinned man. This was highly unusual. Whenever Mac was asked about his former life, he would say that his family had been farmers, and he had taught kindergarten and now was a fisherman. Nevertheless, a light-skinned woman married to a dark man was enough to make the village leaders suspicious. Second, I was suspect because I tried hard to stay clean. Early in the genocide I had cut my long black hair. Everyone had to have short hair under the Khmer Rouge. I bathed often and I fixed what hair I had left every day, curling some short ends around my ears, before going to the communal dining area.

Most evenings after the communal dining, we stayed for a "meeting." These meetings were part brainwashing using Khmer Rouge propaganda, and part interrogation to eliminate those who were hiding their pasts. They would say, "Angkar needs an airplane mechanic. Angkar needs a doctor. Who will volunteer?" Some of the 17 Group would raise their hands to volunteer, and they would later "disappear."

One time the village leader accused us of not wanting to drop "imperialist Western styles." He told us that we needed to follow the "rule of Angkar" and eliminate anything Western from our lives. I felt he was talking about me! I became more careful about my appearance in order to try to "blend in," but I always tried hard to be as clean as possible by washing in the river.

One day at lunch time I quietly went into a field to try to find watercress for my family. I saw four men carrying a dead cow to bury. No one was allowed to use a diseased cow! Not even Angkar. The men were hauling the cow. I remember they had a gun! They dug a hole and put the cow in it and left.

You can have no idea of what the idea of having a cow to eat was like to starving people. However, I had no implements with which to cut up the cow. I ran back to the village, gathered some of the starving people, and told them about the cow. Three women and one man said, "Don't worry; we have knives. Show us where the cow is buried." I took them to the field and they instructed me to stand guard while they dissected the cow for everyone. I was told to start singing if I saw anyone coming.

They did dissect that cow, and took it all with them. They did not save a single piece for me. They just ran away with the meat. The only thing left was the head. I took that cow head and wrapped it in my one extra blouse, hugging it to myself as I ran as fast as I could back to the village. As I ran I stepped on a thorn. I remember that! I was afraid a guard would catch me with that cow head, but I had to pull out the thorn. It was terribly painful, but I managed to get home and give the cow head to my mother-in-law. I went immediately back out into the fields to work while my mother-in-law made "cow head soup." She knew just what to do.

I had heard that the tongue of a cow was very tasty and nutritious, but she wouldn't let us eat that. She told us it would make us very sick, so we didn't have the tongue; but we ate other parts of the head. We even traded some of that soup to ladies who had stolen a little rice as they ground it. I was betrayed by the very people I was trying to help, and I was devastated by that. But within a few days, the man who had gone with the small group to cut up the cow, the one who didn't save any meat for me, sustained an injury that became gangrenous. I remember his infection; when the wound was opened, a huge maggot came out. He died in the little makeshift "hospital."

His wife was very light-skinned like me. Her name was Malis, meaning white flower. After her husband died, she tried to get extra food at the cafeteria by attracting Khmer Rouge soldiers. She even tried to seduce my husband because he brought fish into the village.

The Khmer Rouge were very strict about sleeping with someone other than your wife or husband. I don't know what happened to Malis.

Even though it was prohibited, we knew of instances when Khmer Rouge soldiers raped and then killed young women. My brother-in-law, Sway Tani, my sister's husband, had two teenage girls and two sons in their twenties. At the time the girls were seventeen and fourteen. Angkar took all four from Sway Tani. Soldiers whipped the girls with a chain, and then they raped the seventeen-year-old. When she became pregnant, she tried to kill herself. Eventually she died in the genocide. I don't know what happened to the fourteen-year-old. The two boys were killed. They killed my brother-in-law too, because he was part Chinese.

Different regions differed in their attitude toward the Chinese and Vietnamese. When the Khmer Rouge took power, they promoted the lowest to the top and eliminated the elites. Chinese families were often among the elite and usually wealthier than others. In some areas, anyone with Chinese blood was eliminated. In others, Vietnamese were eliminated. If you tried to keep your family history a secret, Angkar had ways to find out. No one was safe except the poorest of the poor.

At that time, my assignment was to plant potatoes and other vegetables for the community to eat. There was a woman from the village who was my supervisor. We were strictly forbidden to eat private food. However, one day my supervisor allowed some of us to take one small potato each. She said that we had all labored hard, and that we deserved a tiny bit of extra food. We were also never allowed to cut bamboo. However, I had a family to feed, and Mac was away working as a fisherman. After our small team of laborers had left, I stayed behind and scanned the trees. Sometimes young informants would climb into the trees and spy on the laborers to make sure that everyone was working hard. I didn't see anyone, so I stayed and dug up an extra potato. I also picked some bamboo. I chopped a small branch for the bamboo shoots, which I believed we could eat.

I went home at dusk, and shortly thereafter, a Khmer guard came to my home to see what I had been carrying. He must have been spying on me after all. He found the little potatoes and the bamboo shoots. He took me to the Khmer Rouge office where I had to stand in front of a table for interrogation. This usually meant execution for breaking the rules. People had disappeared or been clubbed to death for less. The village leader was there, and two guards were on either side of him. "Who gave you the potatoes?" he asked. I told him that my team supervisor had given them to me. To my amazement, they had put that team leader behind a partition to listen to what I said. She came out and said, "Yes, I gave her the potatoes because she is a very good worker. She never misses a day, even when she is sick." The truth was that she had given me one tiny potato, but I had dug up the other. She was protecting me.

However, they were not satisfied with the story and were especially angry about the bamboo shoots, which they said belonged to Angkar. Meanwhile, someone had run and told my mother-in-law that I had been taken. My mother-in-law rushed to the office, came in, and prostrated herself on the floor before the officials. She said, "Please don't kill her. Kill me instead. She has small children who will die if she dies." She cried and pleaded with them. Because she was an old woman, they decided to let me live. They definitely thought I should be punished, though.

I was punished for the potatoes and for the way I looked by being moved from my job in the village to one outside the village, doing backbreaking work on dam construction. It was killing work. I believe sending me there to work was designed to kill me. There were two "lines" of work on the dams. The first line was comprised of single men and women. They were sent to remote outposts, where most of them died from starvation and disease. Our youngest sister died there. Our "Sacramento" sister also was assigned there, but she survived. The second line was for married people. That's where I was sent, after being told to leave my babies behind.

While Mac was away working to catch fish, I was forced to work on building senseless dams. At the time, I probably weighed about 50 or 60 pounds. I was small, starving, and weak. My job was to dig a hole two meters by two meters, shoveling the dirt into pails, and then carrying them up steps as they hung from a rod spanning my shoulders. I would then carry the dirt and put it where the Khmer Rouge guards told me it should go. I remember how impossible it was for me. The guards were brutal. One day, the foreman saw me trying to go up the stairs with my buckets, and he yelled, "Go faster, old woman, go faster." Then he took out a cow whip and whipped me. I'll never forget the feeling of being whipped like an animal. I don't think they cared if I lived or died. They just wanted me to work, and work faster than I was physically able to do. All I could think of was that I had to survive for my children and family. I could not succumb to the pain and the torture. I could not allow myself to escape through death.

Food was extremely scarce. I remember one night when it was very dark, my husband came home bearing a pot of soup. Once in a while he was able to bring us something like that to eat. When I got a glimpse from the moon of what was in the pot, it was a headless rat. He didn't tell me, but I tasted it and then shared it with the rest of family. To a starving person, it tasted fine. Jason, our little boy, thought it was delicious and decided after that to try to catch little mice with small traps he constructed. He was always very clever. They actually worked, and we would have tiny mice that I would decapitate and skin.

My children provided me moments of fear, but also pride and joy. Coming back from bone-crushing work, my Banana Root baby would smile and hold out his arms to me. I adored him. My mother-in-law warned me, "Don't love him too much."

The first year after we constructed them, the dams broke when the rains came. We built them again. The next year, the dams broke again. But this time, there were incredible floods.

CHAPTER ELEVEN

FLOODS

Mac

It was the rainy season. The rains were torrential, and once again, the dams all broke and the waters spread everywhere. It was a horrendous, terrible, devastating flood. Even the Khmer Rouge had to leave. There was no high ground; everything was under five or six feet of water. No house was safe. I was working as a fisherman and was frequently away from home, finding fish for Angkar. One day when I returned, everyone had fled the flooded area except Simone and the rest of my family. They were waiting for my return.

I am not as good a person as Simone. My heart is not as big. I am always thinking and planning, though. At that time, I was continually trying to assess what was going on and how to save my little family. However, whenever I caught fish, I would try to give some to the starving people of the village. Not many people survived that flood because there was absolutely no food for more than a month. The Khmer Rouge had established the policy of rationing food to all the laborers and families, but because of the flood there was no food to ration. Everything was under water. Sometimes I would take a boat out and try to find snakes to eat. The snakes would go into the trees to escape the water. It was even difficult to catch fish. First the Khmer Rouge and then the floods had taken all sustenance from us.

My father died of starvation while the land was flooded; I think it was 1977. It is hard to remember dates. There were no calendars or clocks. He was 86 years old. We had kept him alive for a very long time, but he had become desperately ill with diarrhea and fever.

Simone

My father-in-law had many periods where he was very sick with fever and diarrhea. This was to be his last. As a family, we were given eight cups of rice for eight people per day, as long as we worked hard. We tried to give him our portions of rice, but he refused everything. This was the end for the father we adored and protected. He would no longer eat, nor take any of the herbs we tried to give him. Both Mac and I were there when our beloved father died. At the time, I was laboring on turning over soil. I was almost finished with my assigned job when a woman from the village came to find me. She told me that our father was very bad, so I asked if I could go home early to tend to him. The supervisor said *yes*. Mac was fortunately at home mending a fishing net.

I still had a few remnants from the medical supplies I had originally bartered for when we were evacuated from Phnom Penh. A syringe was buried in the ground, with a little medicine that was in serum form. We dug it up, but we couldn't inject it into our father's frail arms. We put a little scrum in his mouth. He didn't want to take the medicine. He knew he was dying, and he simply said, "It's my time. Take care of your mother." Then he closed his eyes and was gone. Mac called for Buddha and got permission to gather some palm branches. We had a fire all night for him. The village chief told us to cut one bamboo. We cleaned and dressed him as nicely as we could, in white pants and shirt, and wrapped him with that bamboo, and put a little piece of paper with his name, the date, and the wish that he go to paradise, into a little bottle. After that I had recurrent dreams of him rising from his grave and walking toward me, all dressed in white. I had those dreams for a long, long time. He loved me and I loved him, as deeply as if he had been my own father.

Mia

My grandpa would make handwoven baskets out of grass straws. Everything he made would go to the Khmer Rouge. I'd sit there and watch him make the baskets. When I'd ask him how he learned how to do that, he would just smile at me. He never told me. I enjoyed watching him making one thing after another and was always amazed by what he could do. I wanted to learn so badly... that's probably where I got my crafty side from. As time went by he got really sick. We had no doctors or medicine to help him. I wasn't sure at the time what had caused his death, but I found out later on it was due to malnutrition and starvation. He passed away in the evening. My parents put him on a bamboo bed with a fire under-neath it to keep his body warm until the next morning. The Khmer Rouge had worked and starved him to death. I loved my grandpa very much. He was my favorite. To this day, I still think about him at times looking at me and smiling.

Mac

I desperately wanted to bury my father, but there was no dry land. When the land flooded, the Khmer Rouge left, and the population that had been dependent upon them had nothing. They always treated the population as expendable and left us all with absolutely nothing.

There was no way to deal with my father's body, and this is a tragedy according to our culture. We felt completely helpless. I went to the village chief and told him that my father had died. He gave me permission to put his body in a canoe to take to a high place to bury. Religion was totally banned, so there was no ceremony. There was no incense. As a devout person, my father deserved more. He had always prayed before sunrise; he was a good man. Situations of extreme deprivation and helplessness take away your emotions. I can't remember crying over his death. We were truly deprived, especially of hope. We simply lived day to day, minute to minute. I buried him on the highest ground I could find, but I did not grieve until we came back to Cambodia years after the genocide and honored him properly at the site where we had buried him.

We buried him by the ruins of an old temple. We knew that he had been buried with his head to the north. When we returned to Cambodia years later, we found that the place he had been buried was all dug up. People were looking for treasure. We built a small memorial for him, hoping he would forever be protected.

The devastating floods had not only taken our food; they had also taken our supervisors, who had fled to dry ground. I remember clearly the silence when I returned to find Simone and my family.

Simone

Mac was away when the waters rose to dangerous levels. It was terrifying, but I did not want to move my family. I wanted to wait for Mac to come home. I never doubted that he would return, no matter the danger or difficulty. When he returned, we had absolutely no food. Mac had a canoe, though, so he took a deep breath and dove into the water to find the roots of banana trees. Then he dove again and dug around their roots. We boiled the banana root for our food. I named our baby for the banana roots that saved us.

Mac

In a little boat, I went from house to house. In every house, there was at least one dead body, but there was no food anywhere. I remember that I called out at every house, but there was only silence and the lapping of the water. Except at one house. When I called, I heard a very weak cry. I found a very skinny, sick man. "Please take me with you," he begged in an almost inaudible whisper. I pulled him from the house and into the boat. We knew that to the south there was only water and more water; to the north we might find safety on the "national road."

We waited until dawn after the day I returned, and we all got in that small boat—my mom, Simone and the baby, Jason, Mia, and Mara. We shared it with the old man. It took all day to get to high ground, and there we found the chief of the village with his family and children. The chief was not Khmer Rouge, but he worked for them—in order to save himself and his family. He was always well-fed. His wife and Simone had become friends. He had reached the high ground and they had been saved. But he had left without telling us. He had left us to die.

As always, we said nothing about this betrayal. We never displayed disappointment or anger. That was one of the ways we had learned to survive—by disguising all our emotions. I think his wife felt guilty at having abandoned us. She did give us a "little rice powder" when we arrived. This was made from the rinds of rice. In the old days, rinds would have been food fit only for pigs. But we were grateful for anything. As for the old man that we took with us, once we set foot on the high ground, he left us and we never saw him again.

We lived on the national road for about two days. Eventually, some military trucks showed up, and the drivers told us to get in them; Angkar wanted us in another place. I didn't want to go. It was impossible to tell where you would be taken. We only knew that the trucks were heading west. Of course, invisibility means that you can't ask questions. Asking a question was dangerous, so we kept silent. We got into the truck and awaited our fate. Finally, the truck convoy stopped, and we were told to get out and wait for another convoy. We suspected that these would go to the jungle or to the mountains; we had no idea. Life was a dangerous business, with no assurance of anything but hardship. We feared another transport and silently crept away. Our new home was in Phum Kok Lun.

Simone

We did not want to go any further on one of those trucks. It was too uncertain and too dangerous. So, we quietly stole away and headed to a small house. It seemed to be deserted. I left my family underneath the house, in the mud, and decided to go and explore upstairs. I was taken aback because it was not empty. Someone was living there. However, it was very messy! It seemed to be occupied by the Khmer Rouge. There was a little rice and dry fish, and some black pants, but no shirts. Only men, I guessed. I decided to take a chance, and I spent several hours as long as I could see in the dim light—cleaning that room. I straightened everything up and even prepared some food. Then I went back downstairs to my family, carrying a little bit of old rice for them. I was terrified that I would be caught with the food I had taken, even though it was hardly edible and not even enough for one bite per member of my family. Still, it was something, and my children were starving.

Around 8 or 9 p.m., when it was very dark and quiet, a man walked to the house. He was young, fairly tall, and wore black with a scarf. He was pushing a bicycle, and that meant he was important. Only the important had bicycles by then. I could tell he was Khmer Rouge because of his shoes. They made their own sandals with rubber soles. He was definitely from the army. He went upstairs, and I heard him pacing around. Then he came back down and spoke to me. "Are you OK, Mom?" He even brought us some rice. He warned me not to tell anyone that he had given us food. "Don't let anyone see," he said. He also would not let us stay under his house but told us that because of the flood, there were many empty houses for us to find, from which people had fled to escape the rising waters. There wasn't much kindness to be found in those times. Kindness and humanity are often the first casualties of genocide. However, he was respectful to me. I have never forgotten him, and I often wonder about his fate. I don't know why I chose to clean up his living quarters. Perhaps to search for food? Perhaps to help an unknown young person? Perhaps hoping for someone to take pity on my poor family? Probably all of these reasons, mostly unconscious. However, I did learn from my living through the genocide that it seems to be in my nature to try to help others. I believe that generosity, even in times of extreme scarcity, is the right way to live. What good is it to be alive if you sacrifice all your most important values.

CHAPTER TWELVE

THE VIETNAMESE ARRIVE

Mac

There was no more fishing for me. The floods had changed everything. However, we felt grateful because we were on high ground and were living under one of the many empty houses. The supervisors told me that I had to work in order to eat. And what was I to do for work? Even though there were empty houses, ordinary laborers and displaced people were not allowed to live in them. The houses, it was said, belonged to Angkar, and they told me to build huts.

I guess I'm a quick learner. I had never been a builder of huts, but I figured it out fast. I didn't want my family to starve. Because I needed to transport poles and roof materials, I was even given a cart and two oxen. My family and I were fed according to how many huts I could build in a day. One hut equaled one bowl of rice. Two huts equaled two bowls of rice. I was also the only one in my area allowed to climb coconut palm trees to get fronds for the roofs. This became a great advantage, because sometimes I could find a coconut and secretly drop it to the ground, hiding it for later consumption. I've often wondered how long those huts lasted because I was quite an amateur at building them.

However, I soon was given an additional way of earning food. The flood, starvation, and disease had caused hundreds to die. Their bodies were everywhere, and there was no dry ground available in which to bury them. I was given one bowl of rice for each body

I was able to bury. If I constructed one hut and buried one body, my family would receive two bowls of rice.

Burying bodies might seem like an easy job because the ravaged dead bodies were skin and bones and quite light. But in fact it was terribly difficult. By this time, I was extremely weak. Burying even one body a day took a monumental effort when I had no strength. Also, I was not allowed to use the cart and oxen for the burying job. I devised a simple way to drag the bodies—a piece of heavy cloth attached to the ends of a long pole that I bore on my shoulders. I would drag each body from its resting place to the jungle areas outside of the village. I used a hoe to dig shallow graves. I had no energy to provide them the resting places that they deserved.

By this time, different regions were governed somewhat differently. Some leaders or supervisors were more rigid than others. In this region where we now found ourselves, there was no cafeteria where everyone was fed watery porridge or soup. Because of this we were allowed to grow potatoes. Also, the Vietnamese were getting close, and things were in a period of flux. We lived there for quite a while.. We grew potatoes, but we weren't able to grow many in that soil, and they were not large or nutritious. Five small pieces of potato a day were all that we lived on. While we were there, one of the men that I had fished with for the Khmer Rouge showed up. I remember that he was very ill—almost dying. Even though we were starving, Simone gave him one of our small precious potatoes and nursed him until he had recovered a little. One day he left without even saying goodbye. We never saw him again.

My first priority was always to find food for my family. Mara had become extremely sick. She had a huge, distended belly and had lost all her hair. She was on the brink of death. Every night I would sneak out to try to find fish, and perhaps a coconut. We were all in terrible shape. We looked like skeletons, and all of us had very thin wisps of hair if we had any at all. Our teeth had rotted or fallen out, and our skin was covered with sores. Our feet especially were sodden, with the skin peeling off continually.

One day the Vietnamese entered the area where we lived, on the national road. The head of the village told me that I had to go North with my cart and oxen, to get ahead of the Vietnamese. I didn't want to go, but I pretended to join the lines of men with their carts loaded with wood. Later, under cover of darkness, I turned around and came home. If I had been caught, I would probably have been eliminated. I guess I had to be grateful for darkness that night. No one was allowed to turn around. When we were evacuated from Phnom Penh it was the same. Once you started in one direction, you were not allowed to change directions. And you were never allowed to ask questions. We lived in ignorance, but that night the blackness was my friend.

Simone

I remember distinctly the moment when Mac was ordered to leave us and head north. He had buried a coconut for us, and I didn't know where it was. He would often climb trees to gather palm fronds and carefully peel and drop coconuts to the ground, burying them later under cover of darkness. He left very late that day, and all I could think about was that silly coconut and where it was buried. I kept calling after him, gesturing, "Where is the coconut?" He indicated something that I thought I understood. But after he had left, in the darkness, when I went to dig it up, I only found sewage. It was disgusting. I had to rub ashes on my hands to rid them of the odor. I ran after him again, desperately, caught up with him, and finally understood that he meant that it was buried under the potato patch. It sounds ridiculous, but that coconut seemed like the difference between starvation and living another day longer.

Jason also disappeared about that time, for a whole night. He was probably eight years old, and apparently he thought he would go fishing. While he was there, he heard a noise from the east. We were in a war zone, caught between the retreating Khmer Rouge and the Vietnamese army. Jason heard tanks coming. A young Khmer Rouge soldier saw him wandering all by himself and told him to go home. Jason was young and looked even younger. If he had been older, the soldier would probably have killed him or taken him to work for the army.

Our son was always sneaking out at night. He wanted to help the family find food, and he would often go into moist places to find water lilies, water cress, and snails for us to eat. He was an expert at climbing palm trees, but of course he could do this only under cover of night. Mara, our little daughter, always seemed to be sick. She had no hair, and a huge belly, indicative of malnutrition. Mia was seldom sick; I don't know why.

I was terribly afraid when Jason would disappear at night because wolves would come and dig up the dead bodies and eat them. They were very dangerous in their packs. One day ten wolves chased Jason, and he only escaped with his life by climbing a mango tree. Mango trees have been important in our family. I have always been grateful for the tree that saved Jason.

Jason

I was only five when the Khmer Rouge took Phnom Penh. However, I can remember quite a bit about those years of starvation and deprivation. If my sisters and I had been a little older, the Khmer Rouge would have separated us from our parents, but fortunately we were too little to be taken away. I remember clearly the day that Phnom Penh collapsed. I was supposed to go somewhere with my uncle; and I was dressed in shorts, a shirt, and socks, waiting for him to take me on a trip. He never came! If we had gone on that trip, I would undoubtedly have been separated from my family.

My mother likes to tell the story about how I invented little mousetraps. It is true. I did make them, but I learned how to do it by watching some of the village people. They made big ones to catch rats. I just improvised and only caught tiny mice. We still ate them! You'll eat anything if you are hungry enough. The only things we didn't eat were millipedes and leeches. We ate bats, scorpions, termites, spiders, and snakes. I remember clearly that my dad once caught a big snake in one of his fishing nets and brought it home. My mom cooked it, and one of my uncles got very sick from eating lots of snake. Most of the snakes in Cambodia are venomous, and the venom got into his system.

My dad is very smart, and my mother is very hard working. Of all the child friends I had in Cambodia, very few had parents who survived. Their dads would be taken away at night, and we would hear them yelling and crying. The next day, the fathers would be gone—never to return. My dad was taken away twice that I remember. One day some Khmer Rouge came to collect some of the older children. I wanted to go with them and tried to follow them. I was told I couldn't go because I was too young. Many of those children died; they were taken to work projects where they succumbed to disease and starvation.

I clearly remember the night the wolves chased me. I had gone in the pitch dark to climb a palm tree to get its fruit. I was very young at the time, but I was trying to help my family. I would climb 25 or 30 feet up these trees; and from up there I could see shallow graves, many of them, beneath the trees, where bodies had been buried. The wolves would come at night to harvest the body parts from the graves. One night a lot of them spotted me and chased me. I climbed a mango tree in a grove of mangos. I remember that the wolves were down below me feasting away, and I was up in that tree being devoured by fire ants—all alone. I couldn't leave until dawn when the wolves went away.

I was almost never afraid in Cambodia, at least not that I remember. It was nothing to see a dead body in a river as we washed ourselves. I do remember that when my dad took me out in his canoe one night after the dam broke and the waters rose in the village where we were staying, a boat approached us. My dad told me to get down in the canoe and hide while he stood there brandishing a knife. It was very dark, and he didn't know if the approaching boat was coming to do us harm. It turned away and we were safe.

I remember clearly the day my little brother died. Mostly I remember my mother, who sat beside a tree, all alone, inconsolable. She wept for what seemed like days, and I felt completely helpless. I can also remember one time that all three of us kids cried our eyes out. My dad had brought home a little dog. It wasn't very domesticated, but it went everywhere with the three of us. We loved it. I can't remember what we called it. Just a small dog. This was in the village that later became flooded. The village chief's wife spotted the dog one day. She was pregnant and told her husband that she craved dog meat. They came and told my mother that the dog belonged to Angkar and not to us. We had to let them take it. They chased the poor little thing under our hut and trapped it, killed it, and made dog soup. They brought us one small bowl. But I refused to eat it. Maybe I did later; I can't remember. But I do remember that all three of us sat around crying our eyes out.

When the Vietnamese chased the Khmer Rouge out, there was a transitional period that was full of joy and relief. But later, the Vietnamese imposed rules and regulations—not as harsh as those of the Khmer Rouge, but still limiting our lives. There were also dangers that lurked everywhere. I remember one day a friend of mine found some ammo abandoned by the Khmer Rouge, and he threw it in a fire. It exploded, and he was pierced by flying shards all over his body. There was blood everywhere. There were guns everywhere!

Simone

My husband had returned to us, and we knew that the Vietnamese were advancing rapidly on the Khmer Rouge. The Khmer Rouge were retreating to the northwest. Eventually the Vietnamese were to enter Phnom Penh on January 1, 1979, deposing Pol Pot.

As the Vietnamese army came through, we decided to seize the chance and try to find a safer place to live. It seemed wisest for us to follow their army. The first night on the road, we found a little hut for ducks, and we stayed there. It was filthy and small, but it was shelter. It seemed as if my whole family was sick. Mac was very sick. Mara was extremely sick, and the baby was sick and very weak.

We had to leave our cart behind, but as we started our journey, it was apparent that Mara and our aging parent would not be able to make the journey on foot. I stopped a stranger who had a cart and asked him if he could give us a ride. Because I paid him with rice, he said *yes*, and I put Mara and mother in the cart. The rest of us walked.

The situation had changed! As the Khmer Rouge ran away before the oncoming Vietnamese, they left almost everything behind. It was almost hard to grasp that now things could be taken. When we left our previous house, we took nothing; but later we realized we could pull rice off the stalks and keep the fish we could find. Before, everything had belonged to Angkar.

Mac

The situation was completely chaotic. At first we did not know who was fighting whom. We heard tanks and guns. We had no radios and no sources for news, so we did not know what was happening. Then we saw Khmer Rouge running back and forth across the road, trying to escape. Some of them were taking as much food as they could find and using people for shields. As a rule, the Khmer

Rouge never shared anything with the starving people. This was no exception. January 5, 1979, was the last day we lived under Khmer Rouge rule.

I told Simone that we had to leave. At the time we were sharing a hut with another family. Both families left together. The Vietnamese passed us and we followed them. I had tried to make a wagon, patched together by hand, with no nails. The road was in terrible condition though, with years of rain and no upkeep. The cart didn't last. It soon broke. I was very sick and could barely walk. Somehow, Simone begged a man with a cart to stop and let our mother and children ride, while she and I walked. We traveled this way to the outskirts of a small city.

The Vietnamese had pushed up from the Southeast, toward Siem Reap. Meanwhile some Khmer Rouge were coming up from behind the Vietnamese, as well as running away, ahead of them. We moved very slowly along that road, following the Vietnamese, who were clearing it as they moved. Eventually we reached Svay Sisophon, but we were not allowed into the city. Hundreds of people lived outside the city, on the roads. The Vietnamese were inside the city, clearing it, and the Khmer Rouge bombed it at night. It was here, about one kilometer east of the town that my youngest child was to die.

CHAPTER THIRTEEN

DEATH OF A BABY

Simone

On this journey, we decided to stop at a big, empty house. In it we found pots and pans and a few other items. We shared it with some strangers. Mac fished once again, and Jason and I went into the golden fields of rice and took what we could find. We could only find the discards that still lay on the ground. We gathered what we could. My Banana Root baby was very sick in that house. I could not nurse that little baby due to my own starvation. He had an infection all over his head. We were all starving, but he was almost beyond saving.

We lived with many other people in that house. The Khmer Rouge had lived in a house next door, and when they fled, they left a lot of unpeeled rice. Some of the Vietnamese soldiers told everyone they could go into that house and get as much rice as they wanted. There was almost a stampede as many starving people ran into the house, which was flimsy and on stilts. Jason grabbed a little bag and ran to find rice. I was terrified that Jason would be trampled to death or that the house would collapse under the weight of that many people. I called to him, but he didn't hear me. "Come down, son!"

I spoke a little Vietnamese, and I ran to one of the Vietnamese soldiers. I told him that my son was very small and weak, and I was worried he would be killed. The soldier took his rifle and shot it into the air, and I ran to pull Jason out of that house. "Don't worry about the rice," I shouted to him. "Don't worry! I will find you something to eat." Within moments, the house was emptied of every scrap of rice, and the crowd dispersed.

The next day I knew I had to find food for my family. Mac was trying to fish, but I took what I could find to trade and walked about four kilometers to a village where original people lived. I can't remember what I exchanged, but I was able to obtain about 15 kilograms of rice, which I put in a basket on my head to take home. I was very thin and weak. I remember that the rice got heavier and heavier as I walked, until I didn't think I could bear it. I stopped to rest by a strange tree that had a crooked branch, about head height. I rested the basket there, and finally I resumed the trek and stumbled home, exhausted. The sweat poured down my body, and I had to ask for help to get the basket off my head. My mother-in-law was starving and exhausted too, and she had cared for my Banana Root baby and the other children all day long.

The next moments are indelibly etched into my soul. My mother-in-law thrust the baby, who was very feverish, into my arms and said, "Take him; he is your baby not my baby." The next memories are terribly painful for me. I remember that I had absolutely no milk and could not nurse him. I was frustrated and in despair. When he cried, I spanked him twice on his little bottom and some words slipped out. "Why don't you just die." It is terrible when a mother cannot feed her own baby. There seemed to be no hope, and I was utterly exhausted. I put the baby in a little hammock, and Mia rocked him. But he started having seizures and fell out of the hammock onto the hard floor. I knew he was on the brink of death. In the morning, I took him to a little clinic that had been set up by the Vietnamese. He was pale and got more and more pale by the minute; all the color drained from him. It took a long time to see a nurse because there was a very long line. When we got to her, she said that the baby was not dead, but there was no hope of saving him.

I took the long walk home; and around 10:00 a.m., we encountered a strange lady. She covered the baby with a scarf, and said that if we had seen her sooner, she would have been able to cure him with herbs. But later, when I looked under that scarf, and as I tried again in vain to give him milk, I saw that he was gone.

My reaction to my baby's death was to get very angry. I blamed Mac and screamed at him over and over. I blamed myself for letting the words slip out, "Why don't you just die." Those words haunted me. How could I have uttered them? I hated myself for not having been able to save my little boy. I blamed everyone and everything, and I fell into deep despair. It was a very low point for me, as we buried my baby in a field near the big house. He was only six months old, and if he just could have lived a little longer, perhaps our situation would have improved. I wondered how I could go on for my mother-in-law and my other three children. Losing my Banana Root baby was one of the saddest moments of my life. I felt terrible guilt. I brought into the world a perfect baby, and that baby starved to death. How can a mother live with that? I am still haunted by the memory of my baby and how I could not save him. I am still haunted by my own weakness. Sometimes I dream that I am holding him again in my arms—my little Banana Root boy.

After we left that house, we started walking. When we reached a small city, we encountered the young man whom we had met on the train. Mac had helped him bury his mother. Now that the Khmer Rouge were no longer in control, one could acquire private property. He had found three cows and a small cart. He was deeply grateful and gave us a cow. We lived outside, with our cow, near a wall. I had acquired a rice grinder, and I was able to find rice in the fields. I ground it and made it into a paste. From this I made "honey cakes," which I sold.

One day while I was looking for rice in the fields, I encountered an old lady sleeping on the side of a road. Her husband had died, and she was lost. She was covered with flies and was exhausted and ill with diarrhea. She begged me for water to slake her thirst. I called to a young boy who had a water cart, and I cleaned her and put new clothes on her. Then the boy and I put her on the water cart and I took her home with me. My mother-in-law was not happy to see me bringing home another mouth to feed. She said, "What did you bring today?" I replied that I could not just let her die on the side of the road. We cured that lady, and later she helped me with my honey cake business. She taught me how to fashion the cakes into two colors, green and white. People loved those cakes, and they helped us get to Thailand.

There was one more lady who came into our lives at that time. Her husband had been killed by the Khmer Rouge because he had worked for the government. She also was lying by the side of a road, with her son, who was very little. When I went to talk to her, she told me she was dying and begged me to look after her little boy. Once again, I found the boy with the water cart, and once again I took her home with me. Now we had two more mouths to feed, a fact that my mother-in-law made sure I did not forget.

Eventually we killed the cow for its meat. It gave us strength for the journey to Thailand. We also needed gold to pay for the trip, and to get gold you had to have rice. There was no money, so rice was like money. My little two-colored honey cakes helped us earn some rice and therefore some gold. Mac fished and traded the fish for rice also. I guess all in all we stayed in that area about two months waiting for the situation to stabilize.

CHAPTER FOURTEEN

ESCAPE TO THAILAND

Mac

From the first moment that I was aware of the invasion by Viet Nam into Cambodia, I started thinking about escape. Prior to that, escape seemed impossible. To risk the lives of my family members was unthinkable when the Khmer Rouge and their informants were everywhere. But in the chaos after the invasion, there was a glimmer of hope. I was also aware that as a former intelligence officer under the Lon Nol regime, I would have been seen as an enemy of the Viet Cong if they found out who I was. Probably I would have been targeted, just as I had been targeted under the Khmer Rouge. First, we needed to gather our strength and see if we could find ways to make a little money or gold to pay whatever costs would be incurred by fleeing to Thailand. Finally, we left the city in the middle of the night, heading northwest to the Thai border via Phum Nimith, through the jungle and crossing many mine fields.

Simone

Our passage to Thailand came partially thanks to the two-colored fried dough cakes that I had learned to make. My sister-in-law and the lady on the side of the road who came to live with us had taught me how to take water and rice and fashion an attractive two-colored patty. One portion was green from specially picked ground leaves. The other was white from the rice. The cake was flavored with a little honey, and it was quite popular. People would give me some items or a little gold they had hidden away to buy it. Someone gave me some beautiful fabric and scarf, and I traded them for a small amount of Thai money. That is the money we used to escape.

You could only make the journey to Thailand through the jungle and mine-riddled paths with the help of a guide. The guides were expensive and often unreliable, but you had no choice. A very kind woman offered to transport my mother-in-law in her ox cart to the place where we were told to meet our guide. I was very grateful to her because mother had difficulty walking on her own. I still send money to her in Cambodia! We met the "guide" in a border area of the jungle at 3:00 a.m. We didn't exactly understand what the guide would do for us. I guess we thought he would take us all the way into Thailand, but that was not the case. There were nine of us, and we walked behind him. It was his job to avoid the dangerous mines and other hazards. We had to pay him in gold, and even though dangerous, it was lucrative for those guides.

About half way to the Thai border, we heard some gunshots— like "pops." It was pitch black outside, and we were told to sit down and not run away. I had hidden what little money and jewelry we had acquired with my children and in Mac's hat. We had been warned that little refugee groups like ours were often beset upon by robbers and thieves. When the thieves came, they made us stand up and they examined all the children's hands. From Jason, they took everything. But the other things we had hidden went undetected. We thought they might kill us after all that we had already suffered, but they did not. I think one of the robbers was a Khmer Rouge soldier. He was wearing black and spoke Khmer. We were dressed in rags, but one young girl had on fresh blue pants and a pink blouse. She looked like someone who might have some gold. They took her into the darkness and molested and raped her; it was black and we could not see. But we could hear. They didn't harm us. They were only interested in robbing us.

A little further, we encountered another group of robbers. This group found a necklace my mother-in-law was trying to hide under her clothes. She was obviously nervous, and the thief simply said, "I know you have something. Just give it to me before I undress you!" She gave it to him.

A little later, a third group of thieves accosted us. My little son Jason blurted out, "What, again?" One of the thieves asked him what he meant and he said, "Well, we have been robbed twice. You won't find anything!" And they left us alone!

We eventually got to the border and crossed into Thailand. I remember that we entered Thailand a few hours before sundown. The border was not marked or guarded. Once you crossed, you could see a temple with a big yard. That yard was guarded by the Thai army. Mac constructed a small hut for us covered with some branches, and we slept there. We really wanted to get into that temple! There were many refugees already there, but no new refugees were being allowed in as it was already very crowded.

The Red Cross and Thailand had not yet signed their agreements on how to take care of the refugees, but Red Cross representatives would throw bundles over the fence into the temple yards. We could see that they contained dry fish and other food. We decided to try to sneak in!

Our plan was to go into the rice fields and dampen all our clothing as if we had gone out to wash. Our plan worked! All of us walked right in past the guards as if we belonged there. In spite of the overcrowding, for once we felt a little bit safer as we slept under the hammocks occupied by other people. When the Red Cross came into the yard to decide what should be done with us, Mac was the one who filled out all the forms. I was responsible for finding ways to earn a little money and food for the family. I soon had a soup business up and running. I made soup and sold it for a few coins. It was funny to have coins again when we had lived so long without currency of any kind. Eventually, on July 7th, we were told that we were assigned to get on a bus to take us away from the border. I couldn't believe it.

One lady who had helped us get to the border came into the temple grounds with my family. Then she encountered a former friend, and she left our family to go with that woman. On July 8th, Thailand sent everyone who was still there back to Cambodia. The story of our survival is marked by such ironies. One more day and we would have been transported back to Cambodia.

Photographs of Mac and Simone required to identify them as refugees seeking to journey to the United States, taken in Bangkok in July 1979.

Mac

In Thailand, we stayed in the Nang Chan temple. Simone was always enterprising. She had started to sell clothes that she would sew from bits of fabric. Meanwhile, we were simply waiting for something to happen. At one point after our arrival, we were "registered," and I had to fill out a form asking whom I knew in the United States.

I wrote "my brother, Leng Mith." He was really my cousin, but I thought it would be more convincing if I claimed him as my brother. The funny thing was that I didn't really know him well at all. I wasn't even sure where he lived! I actually thought we would be taken to live in Bangkok. The idea that we might actually go to America never really crossed my mind.

One afternoon around 3:00 p.m., two buses pulled in and stopped in front of the temple. Names were called out over a loudspeaker. We heard "LENG MOW, LENG SIMONE." Simone, who was busily selling clothes, heard our names, as did I. We quickly gathered our family and a few belongings and ran to the bus. I can clearly remember sitting on that bus and feeling such joy. After midnight, the bus stopped at Loum Phiny, a refugee camp in the middle of Bangkok. In this camp, we were processed to go to a third country.

Simone

In the first camp, the temple, there was a big tree. I prayed by this tree that my family would be saved. I prayed that we would be sent to a third country. I made a bargain with the tree; I told the tree that if we were saved I would give it a chicken. I guess I was very superstitious! I tried to sell a ring I had to one of the processors for one dollar because I wanted to buy that chicken, but the man would not take my ring. Instead he gave me about $5.00 to help me! He told me to go buy food for my children, but I went right out with that $5.00 and bought a chicken for the tree! You see, it worked!

Meanwhile, the Red Cross was throwing bundles of clothes into the temple yard for us. I was so emaciated that nothing fit me. Eventually they threw me some very small clothes, probably meant for children. I wore these clothes all the way to the United States. I distinctly remember that I chose a blue dress to wear as we left for America. One of the border agents told me I looked beautiful.

I had no hair and weighed about 50 pounds. I am sure I did not look beautiful, but how kind it was of him to say that to me. It gave me a little bit of confidence as we embarked on our journey.

When we reported for the bus, I jumped for joy. All seven of us got on. That was what remained of our family—Mia, Jason, Mara, my sister-in-law, my mother-in-law, Mac, and me. Somehow, we had survived. We were going to live.

Mac

At our new camp, the processing of all the refugees' paperwork started in earnest. We were called in for interviews, and I gathered my family and told them that they should answer honestly but with short answers so that we could be quickly processed. After that there was a health screening. That was very frightening, because each of us had endured much disease and starvation. We all had some infirmities, especially malaria, from which we all suffered. After 23 days of treatment, we were given a contract to sign for our trip to America. America! I couldn't believe it. I was loaned $1,640.00 to pay for a one-way ticket for the seven members of our family from Bangkok to Los Angeles. I had to agree to pay this amount back as I was able. I did not rest until every cent of that loan was paid back.

**We arrived in Long Beach, California
on July 21, 1979.**

CHAPTER FIFTEEN

REFLECTIONS ON LIVING
UNDER THE KHMER ROUGE

Simone

I have had a hard life, but I am filled with gratitude. I lost a baby, but my other three children survived. I lost my mother and stepfather; I don't even know what happened to them. They were forced out of Phnom Penh in one direction, and we were told to go in another direction. You could not go back. You could not change directions. I lost them and most of my original family; but my husband and I were able to save his mother, his sister, and my three beloved children.

I have returned several times to Cambodia, but I have never visited my Banana Root baby's grave. My guilt is too strong and my sadness is still too profound. We all suffered. We all bear scars. My husband has terrible nightmares. I think he bore in silence all the responsibility and terror of the three years, eight months, and twenty days of the genocide. He paid a terrible price. My children suffered too. They find that few people want to know about their past, yet it is very important to them. Their father and I worked constantly. Every moment of every day under the Khmer Rouge was devoted to their survival as we struggled for every morsel of whatever was remotely edible. We tried to be there for them when they needed us in America, but sometimes I feel we worked so hard that we didn't give them everything they needed emotionally. We were always busy trying to make our way from poverty to a stable, secure life.

Nevertheless, our children are beautiful and strong, with great personal character. They do not often talk of their past, but it will always be a part of who they are. As for me, I have come a long way from the girl who cried on her wedding day. I am devoted to my husband and my family. And I am now ready to visit the grave of my little baby, ask for forgiveness, and bless his memory.

Mac

It is very hard to describe what it was like living day after day under the Khmer Rouge. Yes, there was deprivation and extremely hard labor under the most trying of circumstances. No food, no medicine. If we couldn't work, we were of no use to Angkar. We would not survive long. But the most devastating part was not the physical deprivation. The most difficult, and the most lasting, deprivation was mental and emotional.

When we awoke in the morning, I experienced a sense of relief—and something close to happiness. I might even smile. We had survived the night. We had survived to live at least one more morning. The Khmer Rouge were soldiers of darkness.

As the day progressed, a sense of foreboding would slowly, surely, descend upon me. Would they come for me as night was falling? By noon, I started to feel a sense of doom. As the sun went down, I experienced deep depression. Especially the men, for we were the most vulnerable to be picked up. I slaved from sunrise to sunset, trying to show my enthusiasm for the mindless job I had been given. I ended the day depressed, hungry and completely exhausted. I finally fell asleep and the cycle continued the next day at sunrise.

There was no procedure preceding their choice of victims and no warning. There was no "rule of law." It seemed completely quixotic. Suddenly, as night fell, the Khmer Rouge would come to one's door and take someone away. What had that person done? Perhaps someone in the village had reported that he was not working hard enough. Perhaps someone saw him with extra food for his family. Perhaps they suspected that he was more educated than he claimed. Perhaps they had been eavesdropping as he whispered to his wife something that should have been left unsaid.

We had no information. We had no way of knowing their plans or the larger picture of what was happening. There were no radios or newspapers. Just as they operated in darkness, we lived in darkness. We could not question, or we would die. We could not fight back. If we showed any sign of resistance or any lack of enthusiasm for the work to which we were assigned, we would be executed. Our family's survival depended upon our survival. We could not speak. We had to not only be invisible ourselves, but we had to blind ourselves. We had to be quiet and keep from seeing all the terrible things that were transpiring around us.

I could see the folly of their ideology. If I don't work, we don't eat. But how can I work if I am already starving? I could see most people existing only for food. There was little help for one another; in fact, there was always the threat of betrayal. I couldn't even take care of my own family. When my mother became sick almost to death, they told me, "Never mind. Angkar will see to her. You go to the fields. No one can take care of her better than Angkar." But in fact, Mother would receive no help—no food, no medicine. Their "hospitals" were a perfect example of that philosophy. Those who were put into a hospital never came out! They were put there only to die for they were no longer of any use to Angkar.

Affection was discouraged, but Angkar did want children to raise and indoctrinate. About twice a year Angkar arranged mass marriages. Couples would stay together for one or two nights and then go their separate ways to work in the fields or on dams. Children didn't go to school. They met under trees when they were very young and were brainwashed with Khmer Rouge propaganda. The songs they sang were songs about the evil of the West and American imperialism. I have forgotten the words to all the songs but one; it went something like this:

Clean up the bush

Make something grow

Work is the answer, not love

And so we worked—slaved actually. I fished, but was always terrified that I would not catch enough. On a day when I caught a lot, I would save some in the lake in case the next day I was not so fortunate. I kept my head down. I almost never spoke, even to my wife. There was a phrase at that time—"dam kor." It literally meant sow a certain kind of plant, but it really meant "keep your mouth shut." We could not talk. Talking was dangerous. I was silent; I was invisible. I knew only the silent would have a chance to survive.

CHAPTER SIXTEEN

MAKING A NEW LIFE IN AMERICA

Simone

Most of the details of our trip to America are a blur to me, but I do remember that as we were landing in Los Angeles that night, I looked out of the airplane window and saw endless yellow and red lights. I didn't know what they were! Of course, they were cars! How could there be this many cars? It seemed impossible to me.

We were met by my husband's cousin Leng Mith. How kind of him to take in all seven of us. When we reached his home, he and his wife gave us rice and other food. We talked for hours. We didn't know who was dead or alive in our respective families. There was little information about those who had died and those who had survived. My husband and I slept in one of their three bedrooms, with our three children sleeping on the carpet. My mother-in-law and sister-in-law slept in another small room.

Ton owned a gas station where both he and his wife worked. I tried to help by taking care of their baby. We stayed there for one month, trying to regain our health. Both my sister-in-law and I had TB, and we took pills for quite a while. The children received their shots for school. We were all malnourished and immuno-compromised. We desperately needed to rebuild our lives—but first, we needed to become stronger.

We applied for welfare, which was granted to refugee families. It was a godsend for us as we tried to reinvent our lives. It was very difficult to find a house that we could afford for all seven of us. We lived for a time with a friend for two weeks. One day he told us that he was going to leave the house and rent it to us for $250.00 a month. The house was tiny, but we were very happy and determined to be good tenants. Mac mowed the lawn and I sewed for him. We planted a small garden with chilies and garlic. Finally, Mac began to study English at Long Beach Community College. This was free for refugees, and Mac soon proved to be an excellent student. He immediately went to the higher level of English classes.

I started to babysit for Cambodian families in our little home. After some time, I had saved enough for a sewing machine, and I started to spread word among the mothers that I would sew for them. Pretty soon I had paid back Mac's cousin's wife every penny of what she had spent on us when we first arrived.

Eventually our landlord Jim decided to sell us our home. We bought it for $70,000, with Jim carrying the loan for us. By 1982, I was working in an alteration shop for $3.50 per hour. We now "owned" our home, but we had absolutely no furniture and still slept on the floor. Mac had done so well at school that he was offered a job as an assistant counselor for refugee students, aiding them with welfare, housing, and education.

Two years later we used the equity in our first home to purchase a second home, four houses away. This one was a little bigger, and we lived in the back and rented out the front. Meanwhile, we rented our first home to an American family. Eventually they moved out! I noticed that they had grown a lot of marijuana in the back of the house. Dutifully, I pulled it out, cleaned it, and put it in wrapped and tied piles on the roof of the house to dry. In Cambodia, marijuana was sometimes used as an herb in cooking. I was so ignorant that I did not know it was used for recreational purposes to get high! A few days later, that piled up marijuana was stolen! It's probably just as well. I'm not sure that law enforcement would have believed that I truly did not know why marijuana was so popular in the U.S.

All three of my children were in school, but Mia and Jason were having a hard time. English was difficult for Mia, and Jason was being bullied by some of the bigger kids. I didn't think the school was doing a very good job of protecting Jason and helping Mia, so we started to think about moving to Simi Valley where my brother now lived. We never stopped working, and eventually were able to transition to a new house in a new neighborhood that was safer and afforded us a better school for our children.

Life is full of strange coincidences. One of my sewing clients connected me with my brother, whom I feared had been lost in the genocide. My brother's father-in-law was a police chief in Cambodia before the Khmer Rouge. He escaped to Thailand with his family, including his daughter who had married my brother. They had first settled in Oregon and then moved to Simi Valley where he worked in Micom, an aerospace company. My client knew him and gave me his phone number. When I called him, I said simply, "This is Simone. Do you remember me?" There was a stunned silence on the other end of the phone. Then I described our family to him, and we both gradually broke down and sobbed as we realized that we truly were brother and sister. My brother helped us find a new home in Simi Valley, a two-story house with a marble floor. How I loved that house.

Mac

By 1982, I had become an assistant counselor at Long Beach City College. I helped refugees from Cambodia, Viet Name, and Laos with their English education. I had to verify that they were attending their classes. All the refugees were on public assistance, and they received money and food stamps. After they had attended the required English language classes, I helped them find jobs. I took them to a lot of job sites—mostly nursing homes, small manufacturing firms, and sewing factories.

Simone and Mac Leng at his graduation
from Long Beach City College

We were on welfare for 18 months. After that we were on our
own. Life was very hard, and we worked constantly. I had learned
English quickly, and now was in a work/study program. I cleaned
one of my professor's homes and was paid $70 for two days of work,
doing whatever he needed done. I bought our first car, an old Toyota
Corona, from my cousin.

Early in the mornings I would drive that old car to the beach
and pick up cans for several hours. I could make $8 or $9 by collecting
those cans from Monday to Friday. On Saturday, after Friday-night
parties on the seaside, I could find hundreds of cans, and would load
my car's trunk with them. On Saturdays, I could make $15 or $20.

Every evening I went fishing and brought home crabs, mussels,
and mackerel to help feed my family. We grew vegetables around our

home; we were busy and working hard, but we were saving money and we were happy.

One day while I was working at the college, an African American woman named Pat Golden showed up. Although I didn't know it at the time, she was a casting director in Hollywood, looking for a Cambodian refugee who had lived through the genocide to play the role of Dith Pran in "The Killing Fields." Dith Pran was a Cambodian journalist and friend of Sydney Schanberg, a New York Times journalist working in Cambodia. Sydney credited Dith Pran with saving his life during the chaos when the Khmer Rouge entered the city. After Sydney was expelled from Cambodia along with all the foreign journalists and unable to take Dith Pran with him, he was desperate to find his friend, convinced that he could have suffered a terrible fate. This true story of Dith Pran's survival during the genocide was the subject of the film.

After talking with me for about thirty minutes, Pat determined that I really HAD survived the genocide and might be the right person to cast as Dith Pran. She gave me two different scenes of the script to prepare for an audition at Paramount Pictures. I asked if Simone could come with me, and she said *yes*! We could not believe what was happening! Here we were, riding to Hollywood to audition for a movie!

I was nervous, but I remembered all my lines. The problem came when I was called upon in the script to cry. I could not cry— no matter how hard I tried. I thought of all the sadness in my life. I thought of my baby son's death and the death of my beloved father. No tears would come. They squirted air in my eyes—still no tears. I read the script again and again. But I was unable to cry, no matter what I thought of or what they did to me! I did not get the part.

Although several other Cambodian men tried out for the part, only Ngor Heng and I had lived through the Khmer Rouge. He also had never acted before, but he could cry on cue and he got the part. He was quite a bit skinnier than I was, so maybe that had something

On the set of *The Killing Fields*.
Mac sets up a scene with director Roland Joffe (in white shirt).

On the set of *The Killing Fields*. Mac is third from the left.

A scene from the film, *The Killing Fields*.

Here is Mac holding an Oscar for the film.

to do with it also. He won an Oscar for Best Supporting Actor. We became good friends! He often visited our home to enjoy Simone's good cooking, and Simone and I were devastated when we learned that he had been killed several years after the making of the film.

On the set of *The Killing Fields*. Mac is a double for the lead character who, like Mac himself, escaped from Cambodia to Thailand.

I didn't think I would be hired at all, but they offered me a job as understudy to the main character and technical advisor on the film. Many of the scenes you see in that film are exactly what I experienced. One scene in particular was part of my story—when Dith Pran is tied to a tree and on the brink of death as he awaits his execution. I told them that story from my life—when I was tied to the mango tree and later unexpectedly released.

Mac is holding a Golden Globe Award for *The Killing Fields*.

The film was shot in Thailand because we could not go into Cambodia at that time. I think it is quite accurate, with one major exception. Most of the extras were Thai, and they looked well-fed. In Cambodia, everyone was a walking skeleton from starvation and disease. Suffering under the genocide, most people lost all their hair, also. We could not replicate that in the film.

For eight months, I was employed with the film. They doubled my community college salary; I received about $3000.00 a month, and all my expenses were paid as I traveled to Thailand. The studio arranged everything for that trip—passport, vaccinations, and airplane tickets. Every morning, Ngor Heng, Jeffrey Roland (the director), and I would have breakfast together and talk about the day's filming. Then we would go to the location. Jeffrey would ask us, "Does it look right?" He wanted the film to be as authentic as possible.

I was responsible for hiring Thai people to be extras, and for the "behavior" of those playing the Khmer Rouge in the film. I had to draw on my memories as we created scenes where people were dragged from their homes as night fell, or where they were tricked into confessions during community meetings. David Puttnam, the producer, was always there during the filming. Later, he gave me an award for my work on the film. I treasure that award. You can actually see me several times in the film. When Dith Pran is running to get to Thailand near the end of the film—those are MY legs!

When we returned to the U.S., we worked for several months on film editing. Eventually it was arranged for two busloads of Cambodians to be transported to San Diego for the two days it took to film that sequence.

The premiere of the film was in Westwood, California. Simone and I attended. She wore a beautiful silk sarong. The professor from my college who had befriended me also attended, as well as some of our family. There were many major actors in *The Killing Fields*:

John Malkovich, Thomas Bird, and Tom Waterston all had roles. The film won much acclaim. In addition to the Academy Award for Best Supporting Actor, it won for cinematography and best film editing. The film was based on the book, *Death and Life of Dith Pran*, by Sydney Schanberg. I think my involvement with the film was a highlight of my life. Simone and I both felt that we would have worked on the film for nothing; we have always felt it was imperative to tell the story of the genocide. Dith Pran himself passed assay several years ago in the United States.

Author's Commentary

Mac is not a man given to open displays of emotion. In all our hours of conversation, I have seldom seen him demonstrate anger, hatred, or sadness. But even though he could not cry on cue when auditioning for the part of Dith Pran, I did see his tears when Simone talked of the loss of their baby Banana Root. He was crying as much for the depth of her pain as he was for the loss of his son. When I asked him once whether he knew about Simone's character when he chose her for his wife, he simply said he had no idea. He only knew that her sister was considered to be a very nice person with a good reputation. He thought Simone would be the same way. It didn't hurt that she was very beautiful—more beautiful than any of the women in his village. He came to realize her strength and loyalty. He said that without Simone, they all would have perished. She had the determination and resourcefulness of a fierce tiger—and yet she was kind to all. His father was devoted to her. His mother loved Simone and called her Neang, my littlest daughter.

He remembered one time in Long Beach when his mother accused him of thinking only about himself and being selfish. In Cambodia, you love your parents more than God. This accusation cut him to the quick, and he was angry and hurt. He felt he had given up his whole life to bring his family safely to America. He got in his car, an old Toyota, and drove south. "I stayed overnight. No one knew where I was. I considered driving off a bridge." After sitting by himself for a long time, he drove back home. He acknowledged the need to practice patience within his own family. He knew everyone in the family, not just himself, had contributed to the family's survival. He acknowledged that without his wife, the family would have been destroyed. If she hadn't hidden his identity, if she had let one word slip, he would have been killed. "She was the best decision I ever made."

Mia

I am very proud of my parents and my grandma. Millions of people, including many of our own family members, died during this time. Thousands more were tortured in unthinkable ways. But through their wisdom, strength, and determination, they were able to keep us alive through this living hell when so many others unfortunately lost their lives.

I was diagnosed with Parkinson's disease over ten years ago. As my condition progresses, it gets a little harder for me to do the things I love to do; but I was fortunate enough to find a wonderful doctor. His name is Dr. Robert Hutchman. He's a neurologist based in Los Angeles. He has his own small research center. He specializes in Parkinson's and is actually looking for a cure, not just treatment of the disease.

I will never forget where I came from, but I've always appreciated everything this country has done for me and my family since day one… nothing compares to the United States. I was twelve years old when we came to the United States. I am now 48 and married to my wonderful man for nineteen years.

Jason

I think everyone has had lasting effects from those years. My mother is afraid of the dark and frightened of a lot of things. My dad has terrible nightmares. I sometimes think I too am damaged. My mother says I never had a childhood. I know that I have a hard time forming emotional attachments. I don't value "things," very much, which is strange given that I literally had nothing growing up. I am constantly aware that "things" can be taken away at any moment. Therefore, I try to live simply. I try to teach my own children to respect their elders and to help others with no expectation of reward.

Mac

Why did our family survive when so many others died of starvation? We knew of families that hid food from each other. We knew people who took advantage of each other's weakness to deprive them of a handful of rice. My family was not like that. Especially Simone. We tried to be kind to all. We tried to make friends. We hoped to have no enemies. This was all part of our Buddhist tradition that teaches respect for all living beings. We believe that if you practice kindness, kindness will come back to you. But you don't do it so you will be rewarded. You are kind because that is the way you should live.

Simone

I was young when I got married. My mother told me I was very lucky. Most rich families had to buy an educated husband for their daughter. I cried for two days before my marriage. My eyes must have been all red and swollen on my wedding day. I didn't know how I would live with a man I didn't know—cook and clean for him, take care of his two brothers who were to live in our home. How could I learn to love a man who seldom talks? How could I learn to love a man who was very attractive to other women? But I was patient, and I was also tough. I decided not to give up easily. I was determined to fit in with his family and to work hard. I was quiet, but I was also strong. I was completely loyal to my new husband and his family. I grew to love them as my own, and they loved me. The bond between my husband and me developed slowly. As we faced danger, despair, and starvation in the genocide years, we grew to trust each other implicitly. We could communicate without words, sometimes with only a glance. When we were separated, I never doubted that he would move heaven and earth to come back to us. He was intelligent and resourceful. He put his family above himself. It was a bond much deeper than the word "love" often implies. We were everything to each other.

Author's Commentary

Mac and Simone arrived in California with their three children and Mac's mother. At one point, he had to choose a new name. He was studying American history at the time, and he decided to select the name of an American president. "I chose the name McKinley for President William McKinley, the 25th President of the United States. I selected him randomly! But I spelled his name wrong! I would forever be known as MacKenly."

With the assistance of a refugee organization, he went to Long Beach City College to learn English. After distinguishing himself in his classes, he was asked to be an assistant counselor at the college. He and Simone are incredibly hard workers. They pulled themselves up by their own bootstraps. They lived the American dream of success through hard work, motivation, and integrity.

Mac was the technical advisor on the film The Killing Fields. *He was able to provide an eyewitness account of what it had been like on the ground in Cambodia during the genocide. Many of the scenes directly reflect information he provided. Certain phrases used in the film were phrases he originated from his own experience; for example, "Only the silent survive."*

Mac and Simone worked tirelessly at many different jobs in America. Eventually Mac became a computer operator for the Chevron Oil Company. Their daughter Mia lives with her family in Albuquerque, and their son Jason lives in Colorado with his family; their daughter Mara lives in California. Mac and Simone now live in Colorado near several of their grandchildren.

Mac was able to talk about his experiences during filming of The Killing Fields *and later as he addressed my class on genocide at the United States Air Force Academy. However, Simone had never talked about her life during the genocide until she visited my class on genocide at the United States Air Force Academy. Invited to contribute to the class, she spoke for the first time about the horrendous conditions they had endured, the death of her father-in-law, the transports, and the loss of her baby. Both Mac and Simone became determined to tell their stories. They want the world to know what happened in Cambodia from 1975 to 1979. They want to let the world know what war can do to a country, and how people can be deluded and manipulated into supporting a monstrous regime. They want people to know that kindness, generosity, and respect for others should be values for which we all strive. They leave us with these words about their experience during the Cambodian genocide:*

"The challenge was not just to survive,
but to survive without losing our humanity."

Surely that is a lesson for all of us.

Mac

It's 2:00 a.m., and I am asleep. The nightmare has returned. I experience again the terror as I run from faceless young men in black. I cannot, must not, cry out. I must vanish into the jungle or I will not survive. They are faster and stronger than I am. My legs are buckling under me and sweat is pouring down my body. I thrash out with my whole being against the threat. Simone gently nudges me. "It's only a dream. It's only a dream. Wake up. You are safe. We have survived."

Our experiences during the genocide have taken a toll on each of us, in different ways. Oddly, for the first time, as I sink back into sleep, I am comforted. A new thought has entered my mind. During the genocide, I could not cry out. I could not physically fight our oppressors. To stay alive and to protect my family, I absolutely had to remain silent and invisible. Now I can speak out. I am no longer invisible. I have fought back.

EPILOGUE

Author's Commentary

Mac and Simone Leng fled Cambodia in January 1979, arriving in Long Beach, California as Cambodian refugees in July 1979, with Mac's mother and their three children. The arrival of the Vietnamese enabled their escape.

Fighting had broken out between Cambodia and Viet Nam in 1977; and in 1978, Vietnamese forces invaded Cambodia. The Pol Pot regime was routed from Phnom Penh in January 1979, and remnants of the Khmer Rouge retreated into the Northwest jungles of Cambodia. The People's Republic of Kampuchea was established, with the pro-Vietnamese Kampuchean People's Revolutionary Party in power. However, the international community, including the United States, refused to accept the new government. The United States opposed the intervention of their former enemy, Viet Nam, in Cambodia. For a number of years, the Khmer Rouge regime retained its seat at the United Nations as the "legitimate" government of Cambodia.

In 1985, Hun Sen became Prime Minister. Hun Sen had fled from Cambodia to Viet Nam in the early years of Khmer Rouge rule, fearing Pol Pot's purge of rival factions. From 1979 to 1991, the country was wracked by guerilla warfare. Refugees and internally displaced persons numbered in the thousands as unrest and instability devastated the land. The suffering of Cambodia did not cease with the arrival of Hun Sen and the Vietnamese.

In 1991, the Paris Peace Agreement was signed, requiring Viet Nam to withdraw from Cambodia and establishing a United Nations transitional authority to administer the country (United Nations

Transitional Authority in Cambodia, UNTAC). The challenge facing the United Nations was daunting—a population devoid of doctors, lawyers, and educators, who had been eliminated by Pol Pot. Rampant disease plagued Cambodia, and in much of the countryside fields were laden with mines that killed and maimed innocent children, farmers, and livestock. Demining and the provision of prosthetics became two of the major tasks facing U.N. personnel.

In 1993 the monarchy of Cambodia was restored and Sihanouk became king again. The country was re-named the Kingdom of Cambodia, and the Khmer Rouge government in exile lost its seat in the United Nations. In 1994, thousands of Khmer Rouge guerillas were granted amnesty by the government.

Another major question confronting Cambodia and the international community was how to deal with the perpetrators of the genocide. How was justice to be served to the millions of Cambodians who had suffered or lost their lives? In 2001, the government passed a law establishing a tribunal to bring charges against leaders of the Khmer Rouge. In 2003, the Cambodian government agreed to the establishment of a UN-backed tribunal to prosecute those who had committed crimes during the Khmer Rouge reign of terror. This "hybrid" court established by the United Nations and Cambodia was called the Extraordinary Chambers in the Courts of Cambodia (ECCC). Unfortunately, many of the top-level Khmer Rouge leaders were never prosecuted, as they had either died or fled the country. This, of course, included Pol Pot, who died of natural causes in 1998 in his jungle stronghold without ever having to account for his atrocious crimes.

In 2007, the most senior surviving leader of the Khmer Rouge, Nuon Chea, "Brother Number Two," was arrested and charged with crimes against humanity. Nuon Chen was considered the "chief ideologist" of the Khmer Rouge. In 2010, Kang Kek Iew, Comrade Duch, was the first Khmer Rouge leader to be convicted of war crimes and crimes against humanity in his role as the former commandant of the

Tuol Sleng Prison, otherwise known as S-21. Few escaped this notorious extermination center alive. Comrade Duch was eventually sentenced to life imprisonment. Khieu Samphan, the head of state of Democratic Kampuchea (the term used by the Khmer Rouge for Cambodia), was the third Khmer Rouge leader to be tried and convicted by the ECCC.

The ECCC is considered to be only partially successful. It has never enjoyed the full support of the government, and attempts to prosecute more Khmer Rouge perpetrators have been actively thwarted. Over the years, expert observers and some involved in the tribunal itself have charged the court with corruption and extreme inefficiency. To date there have only been five cases, with two of the accused having died, and three convicted and serving life imprisonment terms. In 2010, Hun Sen publicly declared his opposition to any more trials. Because many in the current government have roots in the early Khmer Rouge movement, there has never been strong support for the ECCC in the government.

Currently, Cambodia is home to approximately 16 million people. Although economically it is improving, the genocide still haunts the land. Unrecognized at first, countless Cambodians both within the country and outside suffer from PTSD and "survivors' remorse." Clearly Mac, Simone, and their children are deeply affected by what they saw and endured. The country itself was devastated by civil war and genocide; its infrastructure was in shambles and the social fabric of Cambodia was torn apart. Buddhist traditions had been relentlessly attacked and families torn asunder. Rebuilding Cambodia has been difficult and painful. The burden of genocide is far more extreme than counting the bones of the dead. The legacy of genocide persists in the minds and hearts of survivors.

Cambodia today has a poor human rights record. While the country is improving economically, corruption is rampant, suppression of dissent is commonplace, and rule of law is not well established. The land continues to be threatened by neighbors' claims to its territory. Nevertheless, Cambodians retain their kind, hospitable, and gentle character, and they exhibit great loyalty to friends and family. The ghosts of Cambodia's past, however, remain ever present in the dreams (and nightmares) of the survivors. Their stories implore us to speak out for victims of injustice and inhumanity and to oppose tyranny and cruelty wherever it occurs. This is the message that Mac and Simone leave with us—they call upon each of us to hear the voices of all victims who have been silenced and to bear witness as members of the human race to our common humanity.

Mac, Simone, and their three children, Mia, Jason, and Mara

Mac and Simone Leng today

ABOUT THE AUTHOR

Dr. Frances T. Pilch is Professor Emeritus of Political Science at the United States Air Force Academy, where she served on the faculty for 17 years. She was awarded her B.A. from the University of Connecticut and her M.A. and Ph.D. in International Relations from Yale University. At the Air Force Academy, she developed and taught a course titled "War Crimes, Genocide, and Human Rights." Her areas of expertise are International Law and Gender Violence. In fall 2017 she will be a Visiting Lecturer in Political Science at Colorado College in Colorado Springs, Colorado. She has served as a Fulbright-Hays Scholar in South Africa and a Fulbright Scholar in Mongolia, where she taught International Law at the School of Diplomacy, National University of Mongolia, in Ulaanbaatar. In 2011–12 she was named the Case Carnegie Colorado Professor of the Year.

ORDER FORM
CALL (541) 347-9882 or FAX (541) 347-9883
Or COPY and mail in to Robert D. Reed Publishers
P.O. Box 1992, Bandon, OR 97411
Or order online at www.rdrpublishers.com

Name _____

Address _____

City _____ State _____ Zip _____

Phone _____ Fax _____ Cell _____

Email _____

Payment by check ❑ or credit card ❑ (All major credit cards are accepted.)

Name on card _____

Card Number _____

Expiration Date _____ 3-digit number on back of card _____

	Quantity	Total Amount
INVISIBLE: Surviving the Cambodian Genocide *The Memoirs of Mac and Simone Leng* by Fran Pilch... $11.95	_____	_____
LOVE AND WAR: Human Nature in Crisis by Rudolf Harmsen, Ph.D. & Paddy S. Welles, Ph.D. $17.95	_____	_____
THE QUINCY SOLUTION: Stop Domestic Violence and *Save $500 Billion* by Barry Goldstein $19.95	_____	_____
House Calls: How we can all heal the world one visit at a time by Patch Adams, M.D. $11.95	_____	_____
Buddha's Wife (A Novel) by Gabriel Constans $14.95	_____	_____
The Physically Fit Messiah: Wellness Wisdom PAST *and PRESENT* by Cal Samra $14.95	_____	_____
ReInhabiting the Village: CoCreating our Future by Jamaica Stevens (Collaboratively authored with many "Voices of the Village")... $34.95	_____	_____

Quantity of books ordered _____ Total amount for books _____

Shipping ($3.95 for orders under $25 and FREE for orders over $25.00) _____

FINAL TOTAL _____